FORGED IN BLOOD AND MUSIC

A story of friendship, courage, and survival.

Robert Widders

Madra Beag Publishing

Copyright © 2020 Robert Widders

All rights reserved

No part of this book may be reproduced, or stored in a retrieval system, or transmitted in any form or by any means, electronic, mechanical, photocopying, recording, or otherwise, without express written permission of the publisher.

CONTENTS

Title Page
Copyright
Dedication
Preface
Background   1
Lisbon Maru   4
Kobe House   14
Houghton's Aegis   31
Working Parties   37
A Change of Pace   45
Escape   57
Interesting Times   65
New Brooms   81
A Tough Act to Follow   86
Last Christmas   92
1945   104
The Final Act   130
Afterword   139
The Entertainers   141
In Memoriam   143
Books By This Author   147

DEDICATION

This book is dedicated to all the professional and volunteer medical personnel at Kobe House prisoner of war camp, who worked tirelessly, and selflessly, in the service of their comrades. Some of them are mentioned herein individually, however there were others who served in the hospital for shorter or varying periods who are not specifically identified. Named or not, the courage and self-sacrifice of all these men remains an inspiration to us all: they truly were *faithful in adversity.*

PREFACE

On the 27th of September 1942, 1,816 British prisoners of war [POWs] sailed to Japan upon the *Lisbon Maru,* to be used as forced labour in Japanese industry. A week later, 828 of these men were dead, killed, as a result of a calculated act of murder by their Japanese military captors. And over the following two-and-a-half years, many more died as a result of torture, brutality, starvation, overwork, and the withholding of medical treatment.

Only forty percent of the men who originally embarked on the ill-fated voyage of the *Lisbon Maru* were left alive by the end of the war. Here is the story of just one of them, Joseph Denton, an ordinary man who found the courage and willpower to survive through extraordinary events.

This is most certainly *not* a conventional history book though, if it is even a history book at all. It makes no claim to cover all the facts pertinent to the sinking of the *Lisbon Maru* and the history of Kobe House, or the wider narrative of all the POWs involved. It simply attempts to bring life to the fading memory of just one of these men, Joseph Denton. Yet if Joe was here with me today, he would, I think, protest. Instead, he might tell me to write about his pal, Corporal 'Flo' Florence, who risked his own life to care for sick and wounded soldiers and was later mentioned in dispatches for his courage. Or perhaps he would single out another friend and survivor, 'Yagi San' Colley, a Royal Engineer the Japanese soldiers nicknamed Mr. Goat, in honour of his goatee beard. Mr. Goat's talented though irreverent musical compositions, performed by Denton and a group of musically inclined soldiers, brought brief though vitally sustaining moments of joy to the POWs, and provoked occasional war-crime resulting rage in their Japanese captors.

Equally self-effacing, those men might well have pointed to Lieutenant Colonel Stewart, whose calm leadership, first within the sinking *Lisbon Maru,* and then later at Kobe House, saved so many lives, until he died himself, worn out mentally and physically by his devotion to his men - a man who, to borrow Winston Churchill's epithet, 'derived as stern an exultation from the proximity of disaster and ruin as others from success, and who was more magnificent in defeat than others are in victory.'

Much of Joe Denton's own role was played out in the hospital at Kobe House, a small room around forty by forty foot in size, where the medical orderlies lived, slept, and worked amidst sick and dying prisoners of war. Though in those first few months of occupation, when so many of Kobe House's share of the *Lisbon Maru's* survivors choked, bled, vomited, shit, or just faded along the passage from soldier to corpse, at times it must have felt more like a Charnel House than a hospital.

The medical cast of the hospital fluctuated along with the changing health needs of the POWs, tempered, always, by the administrative caprice of their captors. The trained Royal Navy and RAMC medics, like Corporal Florence, plus Denton and some other volunteers, were there from the setting up until the final day when a rain of Allied bombs destroyed Kobe House. Other volunteers came, especially in the early stages, and then later, either by choice or administrative allocation, returned to other duties. Few of them are named in this narrative, nonetheless their dedication and service were magnificent.

Indeed, there is no shortage of candidates for top billing in the telling of the *Lisbon Maru* and Kobe House. But this is Joe's story, and every man takes centre-stage in the production of his own life - and what an epic and sometimes unenviable story it makes.

BACKGROUND

Pre-war Hong Kong was a wonderful posting. The cost of living, which from a soldier's perspective meant beer and entertainment, was within their financial means. They could afford to get laundry and other small, but time-consuming, jobs done for them, and for most young soldiers, the living was good. It was even better for Lance Bombardier Joseph Denton though. He regularly performed in the garrison concerts, sang on the local radio station, had a small private income, ran a two-seater sports car, and enjoyed something of a reputation with the ladies, until it all came to an abrupt and violent halt with the Japanese invasion of Hong Kong on 8th December 1941.

Denton's share of the war was fought with the Royal Artillery at Mount Davis, essentially a battery of three 9.2-inch guns originally intended for coastal defence. These guns could fire inland though, especially No. 3 Gun which was high enough to command a good field of fire over much of the ground held by the invading Japanese troops. The battery's strategic threat deterring Japanese ships and the damage it inflicted inland against Japanese troops, invited appropriate retaliation. And for two weeks Mount Davis was constantly shelled and bombed, rending Denton's cosy little pre-invasion work-hard play-hard lifestyle into shrapnel wreaked tatters.

On the 24th of December fifty of the gunners were sent to Wan Chai Fortress Headquarters to fight as infantry. Whether or not Denton was amongst them isn't known - he may have remained amongst the bulk of the men kept back at Fort Davis and the batteries further down the hill, where they stayed after the garrison capitulated on Christmas Day. Two days later Japanese soldiers arrived at Mount Davis and the following morning these gunners were marched to Victoria Barracks, and then moved again to Shamshuipo Camp on 30th December.

Faced with overwhelming air and naval superiority, the Hong Kong garrison had fought on until ordered to surrender on 25th December. And so, Denton marched into captivity ... and stayed there whilst the Japanese High Command pondered the fate of the captured garrison, until deciding that such a large pool of labour might best be made use of back in Japan. In common with other belligerent powers, Japan suffered from a shortage of workers on the home front caused by the conscription of men into the armed forces. So, taking advantage of the sudden availability of POW forced labour, they started moving Allied POWs from Hong Kong (and other captured territories) by sea to Japan.

The first detachment from Hong Kong sailed onboard the *Shia Maru*, on 4th September 1942. This was the first of six major drafts. It consisted of 618 men, mainly from the Middlesex Regiment, the Royal Artillery, and the Royal Scots, plus men from the Royal Navy. Some men died during the two-week journey, the remainder arrived at Kawasaki POW camp (Tokyo) in a deplorable condition bringing with them dysentery, diphtheria, beriberi, pellagra, scabies, ringworm, pediculosis, lice, acne, and malaria.

Less than four weeks later Denton joined the 1,816 men who sailed from Hong Kong on 27th September 1942 on the armed transport ship *Lisbon Maru*, taking British POWs to Japan to be used as slave labour. Then on October 1st the ship was torpedoed, and sooner than see the POWs escape, the Japanese Army guards battened down the holds of the sinking ship, deliberately leaving the men trapped inside to die. A report sent from the British Embassy in Chungking, a few weeks after the sinking, summarised these events with grim candour: 'The vessel did not sink for 24 hours after the torpedoing, and the callous brutality of the Japanese in leaving so large a body of men battened down to drown like rats is beyond description.'

LISBON MARU

Lance Bombardier Joe Denton stood amongst the huge press of men gathering on the parade ground at Shamshuipo POW camp on 25th September 1942, awaiting embarkation to Japan. Like most men he was a thinner physically weakened version of his former self, with the effects of disease and malnutrition already beginning to take their toll. Many of the other soldiers and sailors around him were suffering from illnesses like diphtheria, dysentery, beriberi, and pellagra, and all of them were starved and emaciated.

The Japanese authorities wanted to transport 2,000 fit men to Japan to work as slave labour. There were around 4,000 prisoners left in camp by then. But there were few genuinely fit men left and the British officers had refused to nominate anyone to go to Japan. In response, the Japanese selected around 1,840 men *they* considered fit for work. These men were marched down to the Bamboo Pier and embarked into lighters and then taken out to a Japanese freighter, the *Lisbon Maru*. Over the next day or so some of the sickest amongst them were taken back ashore, and the ship finally sailed on the 27th of September with 1,816 prisoners of war.

The ship was commanded by Captain Kyoda Shigeru, was armed with two eighteen-pounder Quick Firing guns, and aside from the POWs was carrying over 700 Japanese soldiers returning to Japan. The Japanese authorities also failed to display Red Cross markings or to notify either the International Red Cross or any of the Allied powers that the ship was carrying POWs, and so to all intents and purposes appeared a legitimate target of war.

The POWs' guards were commanded by an army officer, Wada Hideo. He was assisted by an interpreter, a Japanese American called Niimori Genichoro, who despite being a civilian loved to wear military field boots and strut around punishing prisoners. Niimori had once owned a fair-ground sideshow in Ohio, spoke English, and had already gained a reputation for cruelty at Shamshuipo.

The senior British officer onboard was Colonel Stewart, though in practice he was powerless to affect any decisions made by the Japanese, especially Niimori who held de facto power over the POWs throughout the voyage. Stewart, nicknamed 'Monkey' Stewart by his own soldiers, was the commanding officer of the Middlesex Regiment. He'd distinguished himself leading his men in a fighting retreat against the odds during the battle for Hong Kong, and he would soon earn Denton's respect and that of the rest of the POWs who now came under his command too.

Most POWs went onboard the *Lisbon Maru* with some degree of trepidation. Few of them truly believed the promises about Japan, with comfortable camps, extra rations, light work, or whatever flimflam they'd been given. But there was at least a feeling that anything would be better than the conditions they'd just left at Shamshuipo. So, it was with very mixed emotions that Denton climbed down into No. 3 hold along with the main contingent of the Royal Artillery at the start of the voyage.

The [cargo] hold was divided into makeshift tiers of wooden platforms where the soldiers had to sleep or sit, whilst the latrine, or 'benjo' was up on deck. It was cramped, dirty, and uncomfortable in the hold, and many of the soldiers were suffering with illnesses ranging from beriberi, pellagra, diphtheria, dysentery, diarrhoea, to infectious skin diseases. And sleeping closely together, as they were forced to do, created the perfect breeding ground for cross-infection, all worsened by poor nutrition and lack of adequate ventilation.

The artillerymen got on with things as soldiers do, with much grumbling, joking, and a determination to keep claustrophobic fears tucked away behind the obligatory brave front. Denton already knew some of these men, who were from his own regiment, like John 'Scouse' Maher, a tough gunner born in Dublin and brought up in Liverpool, plus others who were entertainment or sporting contacts. Conversely, most of the other soldiers knew or, rather, knew of Denton from garrison concerts or broadcasts on Hong Kong's local radio station.

Typical of the times, there was plenty of musical talent to be found amongst the soldiers onboard. So, making the best of the situation, the gunners joined together and trotted out all the old favourite songs, with numerous choruses of *Roll Out the Barrell* and so on. And Denton and a pal spiced up the entertainment with their well-known cameo of the Western Brothers' song, *Play The Game, You Cads*, a song they'd often entertained the troops with at garrison concerts.

Aside from the artillerymen in No. 3, there were two other holds jammed full of POWs. Colonel Stewart and the men of the Middlesex Regiment, plus various other units, were in Hold No. 2, and around three hundred men from the Royal Navy were in No. 1 Hold. And on the morning of October 1st, after another uncomfortable night down below, they were all of them looking forward to getting out on deck for breakfast.

Given that there were over eighteen hundred POWs onboard the ship, recollections inevitably differ, depending on which hold, and even which part of that hold they were in, diffused or melded even more so now those memories cease to exist. And, that said, when the drama began both Denton and Maher were together in No. 3 hold, resting in the dim light filtering down from the hatchway above and looking forward to eating breakfast. Then Maher heard a dull thud at around 7 a.m. followed by movement as the ship listed over and then righted itself.

In such circumstances the immediate and instinctive response is uncertainty plus fear – what exactly has happened and how should I react. Understandably, confusion ignited for a few minutes with shouted questions, speculations, and tentative movements towards the obvious route to safety via the wooden stairs leading out of the hold. Another louder crash answered the first question – it was clearly a torpedo. But what to do about it was a far thornier matter, given that armed Japanese soldiers guarded the exit from the hold.

Battery Sergeant Major Henry 'Joe' Gould, a man Denton knew well both from service in the same regiment, and the fighting at Mount Davis, restored order with a shout in the way that British Army sergeant majors so readily do, and the men settled down to await developments. Soon after this, five or six Japanese sailors, probably engine room ratings, came into the hold to inspect the damage to the ship's hull. The gunners could see more clearly now that the crew had brought some lights. Everyone peered down and looked at the water pouring in through the ship's side. The gunners watched, hopefully, as the Japanese ratings tried to block and shore up the hole until they gave up the struggle and disappeared back up the ladder and onto the deck. Shortly afterwards the ratings reappeared and brought down some hand operated pumps, which they assembled and then gave to the gunners to use. Then, driven by the imperative of their own survival, the gunners went to it with a will pumping out the water in short relays that exhausted men to the point of collapse.

But no matter how fast the gunners in No. 3 Hold pumped, the water kept coming back in and it was clear to all that the situation was worsening. An attempt to tow the ship had failed so, at around 5.20 p.m., the Japanese began transferring their soldiers and passengers to a nearby destroyer. Soon after this the remaining Japanese troops were transferred to other ships, and by 8 p.m. there were only around half a dozen Japanese soldiers left onboard. And whilst all this was going on the hatches above each hold were covered with tarpaulins and battened down, leaving the POWs trapped inside in total darkness.

Like the rest, Denton and Maher had stripped naked and taken their turn pumping. Of course, everyone was getting hot and thirsty. And Maher went up the steps, tapped on the hatch, and asked the Japanese sentry for some water. The sentry smiled, nodded, and a few minutes later reappeared with a bucket full. Maher grabbed it and raced back down the stairs and put the bucket down in the middle of the hold, but when he tried drinking it discovered that the sentry had given him salt-water.

As the night wore on some men collapsed and died from exhaustion, others drowned in the bilges of the flooding hold. Those who could kept going in tired desperate relays, taking short turns at the pumps, until each man fainted from lack of air, water, and food, and was replaced by the next man. Maher looked at some of the faces around him in the flickering of four inadequate candles that the gunners were pumping by. The pale light revealed the filth and sweat, the horror, the pain and despair lit on their faces like some toxic parody of a Joseph Wright painting. But pump as they might, by the following morning, it was clear to Denton, Maher, and indeed every man onboard, that the ship was sinking, and that the Japanese intended to kill them all by leaving them locked inside.

Messages had been passed between the holds, using Morse code, updating Colonel Stewart about the situation in each hold and sharing what information they deduced about the Japanese authorities' intentions. The situation was clear enough though, the Japanese Navy's attempt to rescue the ship had failed when the tow rope broke. All the Japanese military passengers and crew had been evacuated, whilst the POWs were now locked down below in the holds lacking food, water, or even ventilation. A six-man suicide squad armed with rifles had also been left on board to stop the POWs escaping through the hatches. And if anyone could have had any doubts about their intended fate, half a dozen Japanese ships lying nearby would soon make it graphically clear.

At around 8.30 a.m., over twenty-four hours since the first torpedo had struck, the ship gave another lurch. In No. 2 Hold, Colonel Stewart gave the order to break out. Lieutenant Howell then took hold of a butcher's knife that someone had smuggled onboard and reached through a gap to cut open some of the lashings on the hold coverings and pushed some planks aside. The POWs immediately started scrambling through the hatch – and, in response, the Japanese soldiers started shooting as the men came out on deck.

There was a moment of panic in No. 2 Hold as hundreds of desperate men scrambled and fought to get onto the two flimsy wooden ladders leading up to the top of the hatch. This, arguably, was the tipping point where only leadership and superb discipline prevented total disaster. If too many men had tried to get onto the ladders, either they would have broken or the egress through the hatch would have slowed enough to enable the suicide squad to shoot everyone who appeared. Either way, the POWs would have remained entombed below, unable to escape themselves and then to open the other two hatches, and every man onboard would have died when the ship finally sank. But at this point Colonel Stewart called out, 'Steady - Steady the Middlesex [Regiment], remember who you are.' These simple words resonated through the darkness, drawing upon more than just discipline and respect, important as they are, words calling upon tradition, honour, pride, as readily understandable to those who live within the regimental family as they are incomprehensible to those who have not. And order was quickly restored, with the men forming disciplined queues for the ladders, enabling most of them to get out on deck.

The six Japanese guards kept shooting at the prisoners as they climbed out the hatch until they were overpowered by force of numbers, whilst in No. 1 Hold men waiting on the steps underneath forced off the wooden hatch-boards and then joined the others on the upper deck. By now though rifle fire was coming from the half dozen Japanese boats that had been waiting nearby, and some men jumped into the water to escape the bullets.

Meanwhile, Denton was still amongst the hundreds of gunners down in No. 3 Hold, minds working overtime, hopeful and fearful, listening to the sounds of gunfire and chaos above them. Maher joined a group of men climbing up into a section of the hold that they were using as a makeshift hospital and looked out through a gap out onto the open deck. He could see bodies lying on deck, unarmed British soldiers shot dead by the Japanese guards and the bodies of these same guards clubbed to death in bloodied revenge.

Maher joined in the shouts for help coming from the men at the top of the hold, frantic to catch the attention of the soldiers on deck running past to jump overboard into the sea. Finally, they were spotted by Lieutenant Howell who unscrewed the metal clip that was securing the exit from the outside. At some stage whilst all this was going on Denton, along with some other men, managed to get up to the top level of the hold. But then the ladder broke leaving the men behind them trapped below with no means to escape.

That the gunners left behind knew themselves doomed was made plain in their defiant singing of *It's a Long Way to Tipperary* as the ship finally settled down beneath the sea. Though exactly how many gunners drowned in the *bottom* of the hold - as opposed to those drowned or shot after escaping - will never be known. But one rotten way or another, that day the Royal Artillery lost 238 out of the 376 men onboard.

The scene on deck where both Denton and Maher were now, was

akin to what soldiers wryly like to describe as organised chaos. Medical teams were getting the worst of the casualties onto makeshift rafts. Other men from holds Nos. 1 and 2 were going back below trying to evacuate the POWs still trapped there. And many men, including Maher and Denton, were jumping over the side trying to get clear before the inevitable happened. Then, suddenly, the ship gave a final lurch and slid beneath the surface throwing hundreds of men into the sea and leaving hundreds more to drown trapped below in the holds.

Instinctively the men in the water started to swim towards the nearby Japanese ships, assuming they would be picked up. Instead they found themselves being shot at or lured into climbing ropes up the side of a boat to be met with a bayonet thrust.

Maher and Denton were euphoric initially having escaped and survived, though also concerned not to get sucked down with the debris of the sinking ship, so they quickly kicked off on the long swim to land. At some stage the two men drifted apart, and Denton swam on separately until darkness came. After thirteen or so hours in the water, Denton, despite being a strong swimmer, was struggling to stay afloat, his arms feeling like they were made of lead as he fought to keep his head out of the water. Eventually, Denton was spotted by a Chinese fisherman in a little sampan who pulled Denton out of the water along with another POW drifting nearby. The fisherman gave his blanket to one of the men and then took off his coat and gave it to the other. After this he rolled them both a cigarette – simple acts of kindness that touched Denton all his life.

Many of the other POWs were not so fortunate and the strong tides and currents took a toll as weakened men disappeared beneath the waves. But eventually more swimmers, and men clinging on to makeshift rafts and debris, began to wash ashore on the nearest islands. Maher swam for around ten hours and eventually reached a small island. Fate washed Maher onto part of the island where he was able to scramble ashore, just in time though to see Major John Officer [RAMC] get battered to death on the rocks. Denton was landed later onto the same island by the fisherman, and so both Denton and Maher ended up waiting there together for two days along with some other survivors.

Until the first men had scrambled ashore the Chinese had assumed that it was Japanese soldiers who were in the water. This part of China was under Japanese military occupation and millions of Chinese civilians had been killed during the last decade. So, the Chinese fishermen hadn't been interested in going out to help what they thought were Japanese troops. But when the fishermen realised that the men were British, they went out in their boats and started rescuing them from the water. This likely influenced the Japanese military to stop murdering the survivors, since it became clear that there would be too many witnesses.

The local Chinese were poor, but they fed and clothed hundreds of rescued men despite the risk to themselves as the Japanese were likely to kill them if found helping POWs. Eventually though, Japanese soldiers visited each island searching for the prisoners. Naturally, many men had wanted to hide and escape, but the question was where to and how. But three Royal Navy Warrant Officers, Fallace, Evans, and Johnstone, who spoke Chinese, persuaded the fishermen to help them, and the three men hid amongst rocks along the seashore. A few days later, after the Japanese had given up searching, they were taken by Chinese resistance fighters to the mainland and smuggled out of occupied China to the British Embassy at Chungking.

After two days Denton, Maher, and the other men were picked up by Japanese Marines. Ships cruised around the islands during the days after the *Lisbon Maru's* sinking, collecting survivors, who were then transferred to a Japanese gunboat. In many cases little or nothing was done to help them, once onboard they were left huddled on the gunboat's deck without food or shelter, and when men died their bodies were just slung overboard. Then, on October 5th the survivors were finally landed at Woosung [Wusong], Shanghai.

The POWs were left standing, many naked, on the dockside in Shanghai in the bitter cold for twenty hours. Some men died there, adding to the satisfaction of some of the Japanese soldiers and civilians who stood by laughing and ridiculing the POWs' pitiful condition. Niimori, the interpreter, joined them. He ordered that the few bits of clothing that some of the men still had should be confiscated, and went around kicking sick men who were lying on the ground, telling them that they were considered by the Japanese to be rats – vermin that ought to have been exterminated. And, indeed, between the 27th of September and the 5th of October, the Imperial Japanese military, naval, and civilian administration had overseen the extermination of 828 men by disease, starvation, drowning, shooting, and bayoneting: *quod erat demonstrandum*.

KOBE HOUSE

Most of the men who'd landed in Shanghai, barefoot and still near naked, were eventually issued with some vermin infested clothing, though not shoes. Some of them were so badly ill that the Japanese decided to leave them at Woosung. But a few days later most of the *Lisbon Maru's* survivors were put on board the *Shinsei* [*Washington*] *Maru* and sent to Japan. The conditions onboard were predictably dire, and though the POWs were given one small meal of pumpkin and rice, they were also denied access to water, and were reduced to licking condensation off metalwork. Beyond this, given their state of health and their recent experience, it's not hard to understand how psychologically stressful and medically inappropriate it was to lock these men inside the hold of another ship again: and five more died during the voyage.

The POWs arrived at Moji, in Japan, on 10th October, no doubt feeling much relieved to be ashore again. They were counted and miscounted innumerable times - an ongoing feature of POW life - then put onboard a crowded, but relatively comfortable, train and given a welcome meal of rice, fish, seaweed, and vegetable. The train, under guard, travelled on to Kokura and Hiroshima, where some of the sickest of the sick men were left. The next stop was Kobe, where both Denton and Maher were amongst a group of men who were disembarked. Then the train proceeded to take the remainder on to a camp in Osaka.

The men left in Kobe, around 500 in number, disembarked from the train. They were marched, still barefoot, some of them quite literally dripping faeces behind them along the road from the railway station to the town centre, with a few sick men being carried in the back of a lorry. They were welcomed at Kobe House POW camp with the usual counting and confusion, prior to being paraded, and then addressed by the new Japanese camp commandant.

The British Army, when paraded, has a quick, simple, and effective technique for counting soldiers. They are formed into three ranks, the person in command shouts 'Squad [or whatever…] Number,' and the first soldier in the front-rank shouts 'one,' followed quickly by the next front-rank soldier who shouts 'two' and so on. The person in command then multiplies the final shouted number by three to produce a total count of the number of men present on parade. In that way large numbers of men can be accurately counted literally in seconds.

But Japanese camp administrations invariably turned order into chaos, whether by mathematic incompetence or by insistence on bringing their own variations into the system. At Kobe House the POWs were ordered to number [call out] on parade in Japanese, something almost guaranteed to go wrong. No doubt this now conjures up popular culture images, where prisoners are seen having fun baiting the guards whilst on parade in the cinema portrayals that inform much public perception of POW existence.

Cinema portrayals of defiant POWs ragging the guards might, arguably, capture some of the essence of the times in [some] German POW camps. But at Kobe House, the POW experience was, in every way, very very different. As stated, counting had to be done in Japanese, and the consequences of making a mistake could range from a slap across the face to being beaten unconscious. Being on parade, and being counted, was something that weak and emaciated men, who were often physically sick with dysentery and tropical diseases understandably wanted to get done and finished with as quickly as possible. And the often savagely punitive and totally unnecessary administrative incompetence of the Japanese camp administration in this, as in so many issues, was to prove a life and death challenge to all the POWs, and especially to those officers who were tasked with command responsibility and dealing directly with the Japanese at Kobe House.

In addition to being given a lecture upon arrival, the men were ordered to sign another No Escape document. Denton and Maher signed it, grudgingly, but without argument, along with everyone else. There was no point in not doing so, the precedent had already been set whilst in Hong Kong and the consequences of refusal were terminal. Also, whilst getting away from Hong Kong had been a prospect fraught with difficulty and danger, some men had nonetheless managed to escape into mainland China where there was a possibility of finding help from a Chinese population that generally loathed their Japanese conquerors. But in Japan there was no one to help and nowhere to go, and those men who tried escaping - and there were a few - were always recaptured, always tortured, and usually executed.

However, the POWs' immediate attention was focused on the Japanese commandant, Lieutenant Morimoto, a little fat man strutting around with an oversize sword at his side, who would have been laughed at were it not for his life and death power over the unfortunate men stood rigidly to attention in front of him. Morimoto addressed them with a platitudinous range of work hard and all will be well comments, until, eventually, to the relief of all concerned, the POWs were marched back into camp.

Kobe House POW camp was *not* the quintessential wooden hutted structures surrounded by barbed wire and guard towers. It was, in fact, two substantial connected brick buildings, a former warehouse that had been owned by Butterfield & Swire, a British trading company. Next to it, though separated by a little lane or passageway, was a smaller building, a former tea warehouse. Few men had any reason to feel that arriving there was, in any way, lucky. However, despite the appalling initial POW death rate - a legacy of conditions on the Lisbon Maru - incarceration at Kobe House was to bring certain benefits not always found at other camps.

For most men, first impressions of Kobe House's two primary buildings, with their three main floors and a fourth-floor roof space, were less than favourable. The imposing brick-built structure and barred or slatted windows created a Dickensian image of incarceration and severity that events would prove was, if anything, understated. However, tired, weary, and no doubt feeling somewhat lost and homesick, Denton and Maher settled in as best they could, whilst the British officers made ad-hoc administrative efforts to both accommodate Japanese orders and allocate the miserably scarce resources to get everyone bedded down for the night.

The following morning, 12th October 1942, the first full day at Kobe House, brought with it a raft of unfolding issues, concerns, and dilemmas, that would have life and death consequences for the POWs. There was little that was straightforward and clear cut, even tasks like selecting cooks, which ought to have automatically been the duty of men from the newly formed Army Catering Corps had led to problems at Shamshuipo, where some of the professionals had been caught stealing and selling rations. And other matters, such as providing medical care, were to prove even more problematic.

The Japanese [Army] adjutant ordered that a weekly Duty Officer and Duty NCO should be appointed to manage routines. Few of the officers were fit for duty, but of these Captain Weedon of the Middlesex Regiment was in a better state than some. So Weedon took the first week's Duty Officer, whilst a friend of Denton's, Bombardier Bowen, was appointed as the first Duty NCO. The other ranks (ORs) were generally in no better state of health than the officers, though Bowen, a natural athlete, nicknamed 'Ramp' because of his speed off the ramp when running the 100 yards hurdles, was in a healthier condition than many of the prisoners.

The [British] officer in charge of a POW camp was normally the senior ranking officer present, unless, as sometimes happened, the Japanese administration imposed their own choice. This might present troops with a dilemma of conflicting loyalties, such as happened at Shamshuipo with the appointment of Major Boon, who was hated by the troops there for his collaborationist behaviour. Fortunately, this was not the case at Kobe House. The senior officer was Colonel Stewart, already known to both officers and men from the events of the *Lisbon Maru*, and the Japanese didn't seek to usurp his role as senior officer.

Many of the POWs were from Stewart's own regiment, the Middlesex Regiment. The remainder of the men were from the Royal Scots and the Royal Artillery, plus a sprinkling of men from other corps and regiments and the Royal Navy, and even a few policemen and civilians. But Stewart had already won the respect and loyalty of these men, through his demonstrable courage, leadership, and his concern for every prisoner, regardless of whether they were from his own regiment.

There was absolutely no doubt that Colonel Stewart enjoyed the trust and confidence of both officers and men, and that his orders would be unquestionably obeyed. But his situation in relation to the Japanese camp administration was very different. The Japanese had established their administration in an office in the corridor that linked the two warehouse buildings, and Stewart had the unenviable task of being the formal interface between the men under his nominal command, and their actual masters, the Japanese Army.

The niceties of [Allied] rank and military courtesy, for prisoners of the Japanese Army, generally meant little or nothing. In practice, POWs were considered, by the act of surrender, to have forfeited all honour and rights, even to life, and regardless of rank could be beaten and punished by any Japanese [or Korean] guard. Officers, when dealing with the Japanese on behalf of their men, were often punished if they tried negotiating over some task or even for making requests for food or medicine. In these circumstances, striking the balance between standing up for the men under their command, whilst not antagonising their captors, called for intellect, leadership, and courage - virtues Colonel Stewart possessed in full measure.

That said, establishing an effective working relationship between captives and captors, one that protected the POWs - insofar as that ever could be done - would have challenged the physical and mental resources of the fittest man. But Stewart, a forty-eight-year-old veteran of the First World War was already seriously ill, as were so many other of the *Lisbon Maru* survivors.

A call was put out for volunteers to act as medical orderlies to assist the trained RAMC and Royal Navy medics who had been tasked with establishing a camp hospital. The word hospital, of course, is misleading in relation to Kobe House. It conjures up images of the layers of well-resourced medical and pharmaceutical facilities we [nowadays] expect, as of right, when suffering illness. At Kobe House, the situation was somewhat different.

Volunteers were sought from the ranks of the fit men. Though the reality was that by now there weren't any truly fit men. Nearly everyone suffered from some sort of ailment, whether it be scabies, dysentery, one of a host of prevalent tropical diseases, or malnutrition. Despite this, a few men came forward, including Denton who had previously had some extra training in first aid. They were led and guided, initially, by the trained medics, including Staff Sergeant Ross RAMC, Petty Officer Flynn, LSBA Patrick 'Spike' McGreen, and Corporal Francis Florence, who was to become Denton's lifelong friend.

The first few days at Kobe House brought with it a host of challenges to every POW. From Denton's perspective perhaps, the biggest of these was coming to terms with the grim consequences of caring for the sick at Kobe House. A whole floor was immediately filled with sick men and designated as a hospital, and the orderlies' task was to set up this medical facility, though at the same time lacking medical equipment, drugs, or even the services of a doctor. Naturally, the trained RAMC and RN medics took a guiding role and gave some degree of instruction and supervision. But the rapid influx of sick and dying men, a consequence of the disease-ridden conditions onboard the *Lisbon Maru*, meant that Denton and the other volunteers had to surmount a very steep learning curve.

So, there was no training period, no drawn out induction, no watching and learning from the sidelines. It began on day one when Warrant Officer John Jupp came in amongst the first group of patients, and by morning of the second day he was dead, soon to be followed by a long list of other men, suffering from preventable disease and illness brought on by a harsh captivity.

Jupp's body was taken to a crematorium, and the next day one of the POW officers was sent there to pick out Jupp's remains and ashes, using chop sticks, and place them in an urn so that one day in the future they could be returned to his relatives. The Japanese administration also decided to conduct an open-air funeral service in Jupp's honour - seemingly unconscious of, what seemed to the POWs, as the galling irony that these same Japanese were responsible for his death. Regardless, the POWs were paraded on a sports field adjacent to the camp and a (Japanese) Christian priest was brought in to conduct a ceremony followed by a propaganda speech delivered by the Japanese Army colonel in command of the camps in the Osaka district. Then, to everyone's surprise, the POWs were forced to march around and drill Japanese Army style. Unwashed, unshaven, dressed in an odd collection of clothing, mostly barefoot, cold, tired, and hungry, the men had to master Japanese Army drill movements and then, in pairs, march up and salute the colonel. It was a bizarre turn of events that Denton and some of the other orderlies, who were caring for the sick men, and dealing with an outbreak of dysentery, were undoubtedly pleased to have been excused from.

Dysentery - an inflammatory disease of the colon - was one of the first of the many nursing challenges facing these orderlies. Lacking diagnostic facilities, or even a doctor's advice, they weren't inclined to agonise too much over whether each case was bacterial, viral, or parasitical. There were a host of potential causes and the effects, diarrhoea, vomiting, pain, and fever, were all the same to the men dealing with them.

Many of the POWs coming in with dysentery had frequent episodes of explosive diarrhoea. Without drugs to treat the underlying causative illness, or intra-venous fluids to maintain hydration, the orderlies just did their best, which was sometimes little more than keeping the patients clean and comfortable by washing and changing them. Unfortunately, though, unlike a real hospital, there was no outside laundry facility providing clean linen. In fact, there was no linen or any other such niceties, with bedding being improvised initially using old rice sacks and whatever else was to hand. Regardless of provenance though, the flow of soiled bedding still had to be dealt with by the orderlies themselves, as best they could, in the washroom.

Caring for the sick under the conditions prevalent throughout the Japanese POW camps was a physical, emotional, and even spiritual challenge. Of course, different men found different ways of dealing with the situation. A few men were buoyed by a calling, a belief in God, and the duty to help their fellow man. Others, especially the doctors, brought with them a vocation that was often strengthened by the conditions they faced. Many like Denton, akin to Gerasim, didn't overly rationalise, they instinctively did what they did as an act of humanity.

Denton had always been a self-confident outgoing type who enjoyed entertaining his mates. Prior to the war he qualified as a [regimental] physical training instructor, and he was used to having to take charge and supervise men. And the confidence and leadership skills he'd acquired were to stand him in good stead now as, alongside the other volunteers, he learned to adapt to his new role.

Arthur Alsey, a sergeant in the Royal Scots, was brought into the hospital during those first few weeks, and he witnessed Denton's transformation from artilleryman to nurse. Alsey's day started, like many others', badly. He was ill, probably with [wet] beriberi, a nutritional deficiency disease prevalent amongst Far East POWs, caused by a lack of vitamin B1. The symptoms, if untreated, progress to massive oedema and heart failure. The symptoms also include tiredness and a lack of energy, and Alsey struggled to get out of his bed [on the sleeping platform] to go to the first parade (roll call) of the day at 05.30 hours.

Failing to attend any parade or muster, whilst a prisoner of the Japanese Army, could have immediate and violent consequences. Accordingly, Denton brought Alsey's situation to Corporal Florence's attention and Alsey was taken straight away to the hospital. Alsey was less than thrilled at being surrounded by men suffering from dysentery, violently and pungently defecating, not to mention the unfortunate Sergeant Betts constantly retching and vomiting. But, whilst conditions in the hospital were somewhat chaotic, being admitted generally protected a man from the consequences of not attending a parade or muster, and enabled him to rest at least, and to get whatever treatment and medication *might* be available.

However, the outbreak of dysentery did concentrate the attention of the Japanese Army medical services. Their interest was not, however, in any way focused on saving the lives of the POWs. It was just that any infectious disease raised concerns about the danger of cross infection to the guards and to the local civilian population. Consequently, such concerns often prompted various ineffectual and often counter-productive measures, such as a procedure that the POWs sometimes referred to as glass-rodding.

Essentially, a Japanese doctor or medical orderly would insert a glass rod into the rear end of the POW suspected of carrying an infectious disease to obtain a stool sample for testing. The idea being that POWs found to have an infection could then be isolated. This might have had some benefit if the procedure had been carried out efficiently, and if it had then resulted in the POW concerned receiving appropriate medical treatment. However, given the nonsense that the rods were often used on more than one patient and, or, subsequently mislabelled, it was just another pointless and uncomfortable procedure. Though some men appreciated the ironic humour, of respectfully bowing, and then turning, bending, and parading one's bare arse to the Japanese staff.

In general, the presence of Japanese guards or medical personnel brought added concerns for the orderlies, not least Denton who grew to hate them with a vengeance. Failure, whether by the orderlies or their patients, to bow, salute, or in any way meet [what the POWs generally felt were] capricious and unpredictable demands, brought with it the likelihood of immediate physical punishment. It was natural under such circumstances for medics and orderlies to try to stand up for the men under their care. Yet doing so risked provoking the guards further - a risk the orderlies faced as they learned to navigate the fine line between defending the patients without also provoking violence or otherwise exacerbating the situation.

Of course, there was no shortage of issues for the orderlies to choose from - food, or its lack, being an ongoing misery. There's an irony herein, given that many patients had become sick due to malnutrition, in the fact that the Japanese then cut the already insufficient food ration by fifty percent for the sick men [non-workers] at Kobe House leaving them with vegetable water, bread cubes, or rice and cabbage water.

None of the men in the hospital were impressed by the quality of the food, but starving men eat whatever they can get - with the exception, perhaps, of men, like Sergeant Betts (who subsequently died), who was vomiting too much to hold down even liquids. In these conditions, surrounded by starving, sick, vomiting, defecating - often dying - men, the orderlies did their best without medicines, equipment, or even adequate washing facilities, to take care of their comrades. It was a task to daunt even trained and experienced medics, and a huge challenge for Denton.

Of course, individuals brought with them - or dealt with - their own strengths and weaknesses. Denton was a man who had always been strongly self-confident. Photographs taken prior to the war show a likeable young soldier, booted, spurred, looking the viewer in the eye, and ready for anything. It was a confidence and readiness to accept the challenge that Denton was never to lose.

Alsey, in tones that may or may not have been admiring, described Denton as acting and looking as if he was the Commanding Officer. But the brutal conditions of the Japanese prison camps often confounded established polity. It might be stretching the point a little in Denton's instance, but as Eric Lomax, a POW captured in Singapore, whose book *The Railwayman* has become one of the classics of [Japanese] prisoner of war literature illustrates: 'Under those terrible pressures a private might emerge as a leader, and his standing would be accepted [whilst] some of the traditional leaders, on the other hand, some of the senior officers, sank without trace.'

Alsey's second day in the hospital was marked by more death. Edward Butterfield, a young infantryman, died in the afternoon, and was laid out by the orderlies. The trained medics, like Corporal Florence, or Sergeant Ross, had experience and some training in caring for the dying and the dead. But, even in an era, unlike today, when most people died at home rather than in a hospital, it was still a very emotional challenge for Denton and the others.

Of course, setting, even the most modern clinical one, does not make laying out the dead a pleasant task. Protocols differ, but essentially the first step (after being pronounced dead by a qualified medical practitioner) is to have surgical drains, urinary catheters, and other medical and surgical equipment removed. The body is then washed, and nostrils, throat, ears, and anus are plugged with cotton wool to prevent leakage of body fluids. Wounds are covered with sterile film and then the body is wrapped in a sheet or shroud. The nurse does all this wearing surgical gloves and a mask and uses long forceps for inserting the cotton wool into the various orifices. Finally, having been washed and readied to be moved, the deceased is taken away by porters to the hospital morgue, and the nurse, job done, dumps used dressings, forceps, bedsheets, and whatever into various bins where they disappear along a well-ordered chain of disposal. However, Joe Denton's experience wasn't quite like this...

Newly minted volunteer medical orderlies, including Denton, had to figure out their own protocols. First, they had to be sure that their patients *were* dead - there was no doctor to assume this responsibility. So, the POW orderlies worked it out for themselves. Listen, and look, for breathing. Feel for a pulse and, in the absence of one, go on to look for pupil reaction to light. Of course, there were no handy little pen-torches so they just did what they could by lifting both eyelids and using the ambient light, such as it was, in the interior warehouse gloom. Then, lacking stethoscopes, stick an ear against the chest to listen for a heartbeat. It's all easier than it [possibly] sounds though. Death, in a physical sense, is something that one quickly learns to recognise. Perhaps the hardest thing for these young men to learn was how to come to terms with the futility of these deaths and holding in the toxic mixture of anger and grief that came with them.

Warrant Officer Jupp, one of the older men, had died two days after his forty-first birthday, from what was thought to be to be 'asthenia' or weakness of the heart caused by illness and mistreatment. Privates Arron 'Albert' Dixon, and Harry Elliot, were both younger than Denton and they died in front of him in the little hospital at Kobe House. Whilst Private James Myles who was sent off to Ichioka Hospital to die, was only twenty years old.

The day after Myles had painfully voided his last hours gut-wracked with dysentery was Denton's twenty-fourth birthday, a day this year with little to celebrate. There was though, much to reflect on for Denton, harshly disabused of the dissonance from personal mortality that normally swaddles youth and affronted by the innate wrongness in having to nurse one's comrades as they die from preventable treatable diseases.

Putting thoughts of personal mortality to one side and focusing on the here and now, volunteer orderlies had to deal with practicalities, such as laying out their dead peers, using whatever equipment that they were given - which was precious little. The human body leaks after death as muscular control is lost and, as mentioned earlier, the various body cavities are stopped with cotton wool and the dead person, if male, is [often] shaved and has their hair combed as an act of care and respect. At Kobe such niceties fell by the wayside and the orderlies did their best with what they had. So, they used the only thing available to them to plug the dead soldier's anus - a small scrap of rag, pushed in with a gloveless finger. Then, finally, the man was wrapped in a bit of cloth, if one could be found, ready to be taken for the funeral rites. Though the way these rites were facilitated was to prove a trauma that would haunt those involved for the rest of their lives.

Warrant Officer Jupp's removal had at least been conducted in a somewhat respectful manner with his body taken away in a coffin: though this process was set to change. When a prisoner died at Kobe House, his body was swiftly laid out ready for cremation and taken away either later that day or the following day, depending on the time of death. After death though, the body goes through stages of rigor mortis. At first the body is soft, and the muscles are pliable as they're receiving some oxygen anaerobically: the consequence being that the limbs can still be moved and bent. Then the body gradually begins to stiffen, usually beginning with the facial muscles and then spreading to the rest of the body. As the stiffening process advances, it becomes increasingly difficult for someone to flex and bend the corpse's joints and limbs. And, so, the process gradually continues until the body becomes completely stiff and rigid before moving into the final stage when rigor mortis passes.

The speed at which the process of rigor mortis proceeds varies depending on the temperature of the body prior to death, the cause of death, external factors such as ambient temperatures and weather – winter or summer – and myriad other factors. From the perspective of the medical orderlies at Kobe House such forensic niceties were unimportant, until their captors informed them that in future dead patients had to be taken away for cremation in a small round wooden barrel.

If you've got to stuff your friend's corpse into a barrel, then clearly the 'best' time to do it is immediately after death whilst the body is soft, and the limbs can still be bent. The medical orderlies were smart enough to work this one out for themselves, of course. Though their actions were always subject to the sanctions and permissions of the Japanese Army medical soldier, and whether there was a barrel immediate available. But, assuming that the orderlies were in a position to fold up the dead man's limbs and put the body into the barrel shortly after death, the choice then is whether to take the body outside to do the job or to bring the barrel upstairs to the hospital.

The psychological 'am I next' effect upon the remaining patients of watching a comrade being put in a barrel need little amplification, so it was arguably best to take the body down to the small open area between the two main accommodation blocks. The final step is then to fold the limbs, bending the knees up to the chest and tucking the arms, elbows bent, into the chest. String or rope, or bits of old bandage, if available, make holding everything in place easier as the body, held either side by two orderlies, is eased into the barrel. And if nothing is available then the orderlies just need to do their best to hold the dead man's limbs into his body whilst getting their own arms inside to rearrange and push everything together as the body is shoved into the barrel. However, all that depends on having a barrel that is big enough.

In wartime Japan though, barrels didn't always come conveniently suited for storing corpses. The orderlies had to do their best with whatever was provided, often old wooden soybean barrels. But, whatever their provenance, they were sized small enough to go on the back of a pedal tricycle, which is how the barrelled-up corpses were transported out of camp and taken to a crematorium.

If the barrel was too small, or the orderlies were delayed in putting the bodies into the barrels, then their task was complicated by whatever degree of rigor the corpse was in. So, if the body couldn't be folded it would have to be cut and smashed up. Human joints, especially the hip and knees, are strong, held together by tough muscles and tendons which must be cut into and severed before the joints can be pulled apart and dislocated. Then, once the joints are dislocated, with enough muscle, tendon, and soft tissue cut away, parts of the body might be folded up into the torso. An alternative would be to break the bones and sever the limbs completely, all depending really, on whatever tools might be available, ranging from a knife to even leverage and a orderlies' booted foot to break the spine. However, given the myriad possible variations on an understandably poorly documented theme, perhaps the best way to envisage the process and understand its emotional effect upon the medical orderlies, is to imagine the practicalities of having to do all this yourself – to someone you know very well and have just watched die.

At Kobe House, the barrelled-up dead were placed outside by the main gate ready to be taken away by a Japanese workman on his tricycle. The work parties entering and leaving camp then sometimes had the morale-sapping experience of having to march past these barrels. But for the orderlies, whose duty it was to tuck their friends' rotting bodies into these impromptu coffins, the psychological trauma ran deep. Suffice, perhaps, to say that long after the war, Joe Denton, always ready to sing and entertain, enjoyed belting out all the old wartime favourites - but never, never, *Roll out the Barrel*.

Usually, when a body was taken away on a workday when most men were away from camp, Lieutenant Morimoto, the Japanese camp commandant, would make the officers (who normally remained behind) run through the streets of Kobe afterwards. But on rest days he would parade the whole camp, including orderlies and sick men. With over five hundred men, there wasn't enough space in the small outside area between the two blocks, so they paraded in the street outside the camp. Next, with the POWs stood to attention, Morimoto would sashay into the street and the order to salute him would be given. After the POWs had saluted the commandant, the barrelled-up body would be wheeled out past the assembled men, and the POWs would be allowed to pay their respects to their fallen comrade, by saluting the passing barrel.

After the body had been taken away on a tricycle, all the POWs, whether ill or not, would be doubled [run] through the streets of Kobe accompanied by Japanese guards. Given the starved and debilitated physical condition of even the fittest of the soldiers, and the age of the officers, some of whom were over fifty years old, it was inevitable that some men wouldn't be able to keep up or would even collapse in the road. The response of the guards was to beat them with bamboo sticks, or whatever came to hand: Morimoto favoured his sword scabbard. Then, as the final madness in these funerary rites, the POWs would have to run back to camp carrying those men who'd already collapsed.

HOUGHTON'S AEGIS

The setting up of the hospital, whilst vitally important, was only one part of the continuing establishment of a camp administration. Given the lack of material resources, the appalling rates of disease and illness, and the difficulties of working under a violent and unpredictable Japanese control, it was a thankless task. Even so, Colonel Stewart, as the senior officer, had faced up to this responsibility in his usual determined manner.

Stewart, a forty-eight-year-old veteran of the First World War, was visibly unwell. Nonetheless, he continued doing what he could on behalf of the POWs, protesting orders such as having to learn Japanese Army [parade] drill and so on. But with Stewart's worsening illness, and the illness of other senior officers, including Majors Innes and Pitt, in practice command often fell to other, and more junior, officers including Captain Weeden.

The officers sought official help for the medical orderlies who were overwhelmed, in those first weeks, with the number of patients. In response, around the 19th October, the Japanese administration dispatched some sick men to Ichioka, a POW hospital at [nearby] Osaka Stadium. This hospital was little or no better equipped than Kobe House, though at least there was a doctor there, Lieutenant Jackson. However even Jackson, who was nigh venerated by the POWs for his struggles on behalf of his patients, was unable to save all the Kobe House men, some of whom died shortly after arrival.

Anyhow, the following day, Colonel Stewart along with some others of the sickest of the sick was taken in the back of a crammed open lorry, to the POW hospital at Ichioka. He looked desperately ill, though was trying hard, as one of his officers observed, not to show it. Less than twenty-four hours later, he was dead.

It's said that he is blessed who dies not late but well, though probably not by Stewart or any other unfortunate experiencing death from dehydration and painful bloody diarrhoea. Regardless, his men certainly seemed to feel that he had *lived* well, and news of his loss hit them hard. And understandably, as Maher commented bitterly, the POWs blamed the Japanese administration for what they considered to be Stewart's murder.

The Colonel's death was only one of many traumas marking the birth of Kobe House, and in literal terms, not even the worst of them, though perhaps it marked the nadir from which resistance sprang. Fighting back against Imperial Japanese prison polity, though, was not like some feel-good Hollywood movie game of 'goon baiting and sabotage' played out between POWs and guards: though these things were certainly set to happen, and Denton was to be involved in much of it. For individual prisoners at Kobe House though, perhaps the greatest act of defiance was just *not* to die.

Death was the essence of the Imperial Japanese Army's own code of conduct, which was harsh and unequivocal: a soldier should never surrender – should 'never live to experience shame as a prisoner.' That they themselves truly lived up (no pun intended) to this part of the code is indisputable. But Denton and the other men who had embarked on the *Lisbon Maru*, a month or so previously, were cast from a very different cultural mould. They had played their part in the battle for Hong Kong, fighting against overwhelming odds until being ordered to surrender – to die pointlessly there onwards was no part of their beliefs.

Regrettably, the more admirable part of the Japanese military code, that they should show mercy to those who surrendered to them, had long sunk without trace in the waves of barbarity that accompanied militarism and victory. Nonetheless, when viewed from the uniquely Japanese-military perspective, much of what was to happen at Kobe House made sense. Denton, Florence, Maher, Colonel Stewart, and indeed every single man incarcerated there, had given up – had *surrendered* – their right to even exist. So, unworthy of life, they had no need of food, they had no right to decent treatment, nor was there any point in giving medical care to sustain the sick and dying.

In the face of this logic, Denton did what he could for himself, as an individual, to survive – to endure, either to fight again or return to home and family. He also did what he could, as a medical orderly, and later as an entertainer, to help others achieve the same. Yet paradoxically, to survive as an individual one needed to be part of a group, both as small groups of mutually supportive mates and as part of the larger group – a cohesive disciplined military organisation.

Survival as an individual, springs from the individual, and it's a well-accepted fact that, in extremis, the *will* to survive is paramount. Of course, this certainly doesn't mean that men who succumbed to overwhelming starvation, disease and illness, or physical brutality, were in any way to blame for their own death: sometimes no amount of determination will sustain life. But many POWs felt that sometimes a man, overwhelmed, physically and mentally, died really because he had given up the struggle to live.

Age, strength, even rank and social background, underpinned and informed one's mental attitude at Kobe House. Arriving there young, and [relatively] strong, like Denton, or already inured to hardship, as were so many men from impoverished backgrounds, was a sort of benefit. Older men, in some ways were at a disadvantage - less physically resilient, though experience and maturity could compensate. Whilst men from wealthier backgrounds sometimes, though by no means always, found adjusting to POW life harder than did their less privileged peers. Though in the absolute, all such things conferred neither sentence nor magic formula.

Denton had been born in Middlesex, a month or so before the end of the First World War, though mostly brought up in Rotherham in the north of England. Unlike many of the other ranks at Kobe House, Denton's family had reaped the benefits of the postwar economic boom. And as a 1920s schoolboy, his mother's success as a theatrical entertainer continued to provide a prosperous childhood even during the hardships of the economic slump that grew into the Great Depression of the 1930s. Surely then, to have missed out on the tough childhood of privation, physical hardship, and poor diet, that many of the other regular soldiers had experienced, would be enviable in the normal course of things, would it not. But as a training ground for Kobe House, a background of poverty was not without merit.

Denton was a little different in another way too, though now a regular soldier, he was also a semi-professional musician and singer. Of course, he had grown-up in an age when home media was limited to the radio, or 'wireless', when many people learned an instrument, and most people could sing and make their own entertainment. And so many of the other POWs had musical skills too. But Denton was especially talented, and even recently whilst serving as a soldier he'd developed a reputation appearing in concerts and broadcasting on Hong Kong radio. But, whilst Denton wasn't cast in quite the same mould as his regular army peers, he was tough nonetheless, and he was also a gregarious character who made friends easily. And, in the difficult proving ground of the camp hospital, Denton very quickly earned respect and established the friendships that would sustain him through hard times ahead.

As vital as these groups of mutually supportive friends were, the POWs also looked to their officers to establish a camp regime and administration as a buffer between them and the Japanese command. Of course, Denton was offered no say in the running of the camp administration, nor would he have expected it. In German POW camps in occupied Europe, Allied POWs were usually segregated from their officers - so they formed their own, sometimes elected, POW camp administrations. But this was not generally so in Japanese POW camps, and certainly not the case at Kobe House.

So, with the death of Colonel Stewart, and the debilitating illnesses affecting most officers, the task of heading the POW administration was assigned to another World War One veteran, Alfred Houghton, a Captain [later Major] in the Royal Engineers. Houghton, only a few weeks away from his forty-ninth birthday, was far from well himself, and suffering from recurrent bouts of beriberi. Representing the soldiers under his command and dealing with the Japanese administration, headed by Lieutenant [later Captain] Yasuji Morimoto, was a task that would have daunted any man. Succeeding in this challenge was to require a new style of leadership – one that would not be without controversy.

Major Houghton, in common with most any military officer, no doubt began his career with ambitions to command – like every officer, he had trained for it and, when the opportunity came, he was expected to be able to do it. But, command at Kobe House was a poison chalice. Houghton was ultimately responsible for the welfare, discipline, and management of the men under his nominal charge. The reality though, was that he was unable to make effective decisions about pretty much anything without getting Japanese approval.

Houghton's men were, quite literally, slowly starving to death. Disease and illness, exacerbated by the withholding of medical supplies, was decimating the ranks of his command. Brutality and physical punishments were an ever present, even daily, reality. Their quarters were cramped and overcrowded, toilet facilities were grossly inadequate, issued clothing was lice-ridden, and footwear was worn out and ill-fitting. It would be possible to go on, but the point is that it was Houghton's clear and unequivocal duty as a commanding officer to protest these conditions on his men's behalf and do all within his power to ameliorate their lot. But, and a big but, protests might on occasion be met somewhat positively by a Japanese camp administration: yet such protests were often just as likely to exacerbate already dire situations and incur hardening attitudes and even physical violence.

It might well have been argued that if Houghton's protection, as a commander under the Japanese, was so limited, why offer continuing military obedience and loyalty. And, there were cases [elsewhere] where Allied officers' *actual* control of the POWs under their command was tenuous indeed. Of course, Denton, like many of his mates, was a regular soldier with a deeply instilled sense of discipline. But Houghton wasn't one of 'their' officers - not one of the Royal Scots, not a Gunner, nor a Middlesex like Colonel Stewart. And some men there were 'hostilities only' servicemen, sometimes with limited military experience prior to capture, who at times struggled to see the point in submitting to continuing military discipline and organisation.

But only time would tell if Houghton could construct a shield fit for purpose. Meanwhile, the duty of the POWs was to support him both collectively and individually, and in Denton's case, his way of doing this was to be as a medical volunteer and an entertainer.

WORKING PARTIES

For the professional medics like Staff Sergeant Ross, or Sick Berth Petty Officer Flynn, working in the hospital was their military duty, and they soldiered on without complaint, though in Ross's case he became so sick that he died there too.

Denton did have a choice about working in the hospital though. Like the rest of the POWs, Denton was slowly but surely starving to death. This left the volunteer medical orderlies with a dilemma, because by continuing to work in the hospital they lost the opportunity to steal food whilst on outside working parties. But choosing to remain in the hospital would allow Denton to continue working alongside his friend, Corporal Florence, and such things were hugely important given that the mutually supportive bonds of friendship actively helped keep men alive at Kobe House.

It was increasingly clear to all the POWs that they would soon be taken out of camp to work, in some capacity, for Japanese industry. The signs were clear, the fitter men were already being physically trained – taken out onto the nearby sports field and forced to run up and down carrying sandbags. Anyway, it was no secret that the only reason for their relocation to Japan was to provide labour for Japanese industry.

Denton knew that being on outside working parties *sometimes* offered the opportunity to obtain food or something else that might then be traded for food. Indeed, most of Denton's pals, Bowen, Maher, Inglis, Colley, and the rest, would soon be fully engaged in trying to get themselves allocated to the best jobs and factories – the definition of best being those that offered the maximum pilfering opportunities in return for the least arduous and dangerous work, with the occasional chance for some sabotage being a bonus prize.

Kobe being a port city, and the gateway for substantial wartime imports and exports, led to many POWs being used as dock labour. Unloading ships, whilst often heavy and dangerous work for men in ill-health, sometimes offered access to food stocks. The alternative, working in a factory, might sometimes offer physically easier work plus whatever rations the factory saw fit to provide. The pros and cons of working in differing locations though, whilst never entirely predictable, and most definitely never guaranteed, were something that individual POWs soon learned about and tried to navigate to their own best interest.

The Japanese camp administration initially deployed men at random regardless of their physical suitability for hard labour, or medical status. Houghton's administration's policy was to push towards gaining control of work allocation from the Japanese, so that men could be given choices where it was possible, whilst also preventing the Darwinian survival of the fittest ethos that (in certain POW camps) exacerbated an already dire situation.

Denton, sticking with the decision to work as a medical orderly, found himself cut off from the opportunity to steal extra food. Of course, this applied equally to the other volunteer orderlies and the RAMC medics. And to make matters worse, the orderlies and other camp admin staff had their rations cut by fifty percent. Though the POWs were conscious of this, and most men took steps when they could to pass on a share of smuggled food to the hospital both for the benefit of the sick and the orderlies.

All the other ranks (ORs) worked outside camp, aside from those few men who were excused for duties with the camp administration, or the sick in hospital. The officers, however, were not forced to work outside, though those who didn't volunteer to do so also had their rations cut by fifty percent. The officers did, though, receive a better pro rata allocation during the infrequent issue of Red Cross parcels to the POWs.

The Japanese authorities, in one of their rare nods to the Geneva Conventions paid the POWs a small wage, seemingly unconscious of the criminal irony of paying men whilst at the same time slowly starving them to death. Nonetheless, these small sums of money could be used either to buy food from the Japanese or to buy food from those other POWs who were successful in smuggling food back into Kobe House.

The officers were paid more than the ORs, though the sums involved varied dependent on rank. Going down the scale, the senior NCOs were paid 25 Sen, whilst Denton, as a Lance Bombardier, received 15 Sen – slightly more than the private soldiers who received 10 Sen. Denton's patients in the hospital though, were paid nothing and their scale of rations were still reduced by fifty percent – actions the Japanese prison administration justified by the logic that sick and dying men needed less food and also that as they were no longer employed, they were not entitled to wages.

Lance Corporal Avery White was one of the many who did his best, on an individual basis, to supplement the somewhat byzantine rationing and pay system by pilfering. He also enjoyed taking what revenge he could on his captors by minor acts of sabotage. Like Denton, he was a pre-war regular soldier, though from a very different, and economically poorer, social background. Regardless, both men shared a strong sense of 'fair play' and the soldiers' rough and ready compassion for the sick and vulnerable, something that would bring them together at Kobe House.

White, better known as 'Blanco' to his mates, soon found himself on one of the working parties. These men were marched out of camp every day and taken to various workplaces. For instance, some men were taken to the Yoshihara factory where they helped extract oil from peanuts (for use by the Imperial Japanese Army Air Force), whilst others went to a jam factory. Venues like this were popular in that they offered a chance to get access to food – and food, any food, was a driving obsession to these men.

Norman Colley, a Dunkirk veteran, whose inventiveness stretched far beyond musical composition, was the gang leader of a group of engineers at the Yoshihara factory where he proved himself to be a skilled saboteur. Given the importance of aviation oil to the Japanese war effort, guards watched both POWs and civilian employees ceaselessly to try to prevent them looting [eating] the raw materials, and harsh punishments were meted out to anyone caught. One way that Colley's team got around this was to solder false bottoms onto some of the POWs' water bottles which they then used to smuggle peanut oil back to Kobe House. More importantly though, Colley and the four engineers in his team gradually sabotaged so many key items of machinery that by the later stages of the war the factory virtually ceased production. And they successfully hoodwinked the management by enthusiastically fabricating replacement parts for the machines that they had sabotaged, though most of the parts were designed to quickly fail.

Other assignments such going to the docks and working as stevedores, also had pros and cons for those men sent there. The POWs' duties varied, sometimes offering good opportunities in the railyards loading rail carriages with food, whilst at other times it might entail nothing better than hard dirty energy draining physical slog unloading rubber from ships and so on.

Hunger is wonderfully character building though, in that most inmates of Kobe House, regardless of social class and pre-war occupation, developed into accomplished thieves and opportunists. For some of the reservists, such as Hong Kong bankers and merchants from relatively privileged socio-economic backgrounds, such things may have been something of an unexpected education. But most regular soldiers like White, skilled at navigating the complexities of Army life, took to it like a duck to water – whilst those who didn't stepped that little bit closer to starvation and death. Denton, of course, being stationed in the hospital missed the opportunities to steal food, but was spared the entry fee of hard labour, plus the stress and danger that always attended pilfering from the Japanese. Though it was a decision that the POW body politic appreciated – voting by a majority to share their official food allocation with the hospital staff. And that appreciation was also expressed in the form of stolen food which they smuggled into camp and shared with the patients and orderlies.

Naturally, the POWs would eat anything they could find whilst out working, taking great care, of course, to only do so if they were out of sight of the Japanese Army guards or civilian foremen. This was risky enough, as the punishments for being caught could range from a few slaps across the face to broken bones and being beaten senseless. However, smuggling food into camp increased the risks exponentially.

Despite the dangers, many of the POWs tried to bring food back into camp. But they were often searched by the Japanese gate guards. Given their limited options for hiding places, it was far from easy concealing anything remotely substantial and many men gave up the struggle in the face of the beatings that sprang from discovery. White, however, was one of those who kept pushing the boundaries by searching for ever more ingenious, albeit risky, hiding places. For instance, improvised fabric 'crutch bags' were filled with sugar, tea, or whatever they could get their hands on, and the POWs then had to try to walk normally and not give the game away.

Some POWs, including White, were issued Japanese slippers in lieu of proper work boots. Whilst not exactly ideal for protecting the feet of men engaged in heavy industrial work, they did prove to have one unique benefit. Those POWs willing to take a gamble found that the slippers were large enough and flexible enough to conceal a tin of [stolen] sardines inside whilst they marched back to camp. Walking any distance with two tins of sardines hidden under one's feet must be as painful as it sounds, but it was a risk and a discomfort that White, and others, felt to be well worthwhile when they saw the smiles on the sick men's faces after the smuggled tins were distributed in the hospital.

White, Denton, the POWs in general, created their own codes of honour and behaviour – steal [from the Japanese] to survive, share with your own small group of pals, and give some to the sick in the hospital. And, if the Japanese guards caught anyone with food, you take whatever punishments they dished out and never ever inform on your comrades. Though in the hospital they had to become adept at hiding the evidence. Whether it was disposing of an empty tin, or surreptitiously getting a little warm water from the cooks to make a brew from smuggled tea, or any of the myriad other daily struggles to sustain life, ways had to be found – that's how they got by. But living the way they did, the quiet desperation of survival within a brutal murderous regime, breeds visceral depths of anger and hatred. Some men held it festering within them until the day they died. Others, Denton for one, were able to [later] find some degree of closure, or even forgiveness, though more so for the ordinary Japanese people rather than the military. But at the time, they were all far more interested in finding some way to hit back than in worrying about being understanding.

Denton and the other orderlies had little or no opportunity to cause actual physical damage, so they looked to find subtler ways to vent spleen later-on into their captivity. But it was a very different story for the working parties, in direct contact with ships, trains, and industrial processes. For White, sabotage turned into something of a game – a dangerous game, but one that gave a deal of satisfaction.

On one occasion three men on White's working party had constant diarrhoea. Such ailments were commonplace, and the Japanese administration refused permission for the hospitalisation and treatment that the men ought to have received. The party was engaged in loading bags of seaweed onto a goods train. So, keeping a very watchful eye open for the guards, or the Japanese civilian foreman, they opened-up bags of seaweed and sat the sick men on top. After a while they would take the men off and then sew or tie up the bags. Then the bags were put on the train as part of a cargo of food for the Japanese army, with some 'added British flavour!'

Such things might jar with twenty-first-century sensibilities. But soldier's humour tends to be a little rough and ready at the best of times. And these times were far from the best for Denton, Florence, the sick men starving and dying in the hospital, or for White and pals doing hard labour on a meagre diet of factory floor rice sweepings contaminated with rat-droppings. Another time White was put to work loading goods wagons. The cargo included some beer. Regardless of the risks, it was too good an opportunity to miss. So, they drank some of the beer and poured away the remainder, and then replaced it with, as White phrased it, 'Tommy Piss.'

Of course, such things did nothing to harm the Japanese war industry. Even the effects of more tangible sabotage such as putting acid in a train's wheel box, jamming doors, damaging machinery, putting sand in petrol tanks, and so on, though very real, was of limited value when viewed through the macro-lens of the overall Japanese war economy. Perhaps the true value came from enabling the POWs to keep fighting back, to remain 'soldiers', to hold on to their self-respect, regardless of the degrading conditions and treatment forced upon them. The will to survive, that which kept a man soldiering on when his body, worn out from disease and malnutrition, was ready to give up on life, sprang from such things. Keeping this in mind, imagine skeletal patients lying in the hospital listening to the latest accounts from the work parties, laughing as they envisage the look of surprise on some Japanese soldier's face as he opens a beer bottle and takes a swig of Tommy Piss – such things were worth their weight in gold.

However, on one occasion White was caught out in some misdemeanour. As punishment, his captors had a coffin shaped hole dug into the ground, and then put White inside and placed wooden boards over the top. The grave was placed where [during the daytime] other soldiers had to walk over it. Though whilst it's not clear [now] how many days he was left buried there, it clearly didn't break either his spirit or his sense of humour - as the soldiers walked over the boards, his pal, Corporal Reg Cotton, could hear him singing the popular song 'McDougall, McNab, and Mackay, strolling along together'. Yes, playing 'games' with the Japanese Army could turn out very nasty indeed.

A CHANGE OF PACE

Denton was far from unique in feeling the claustrophobic monotony of incarceration. New faces helped relieve the monotony though, and, perhaps more importantly, brought news of the war and of the wider world. Amongst the first of these was a party of American officers and enlisted men who arrived at Kobe House in the later part of October [1942].

The American POWs were led by Lieutenant Colonel Franklin Fliniau, a thirty-three-year-old infantry officer. They had arrived in Osaka after a most atypical voyage from the Philippines, that was the polar-opposite of Denton's experience – only fifty POWs onboard, who were well fed, well treated, and allowed to remain up on deck.

They were soon brought back down to reality at Kobe House where they were robbed of most of the personal belongings they'd brought with them, made to go through the usual bowing and scraping to Morimoto and his staff, generally slapped and beaten around, and then informed that they were still alive only due to the gracious generosity of the Emperor. Fliniau's share of the humiliation was a little more personalised though. Strictly speaking, as a Lieutenant Colonel, Fliniau was now the senior ranking Allied officer at Kobe House, and he ought to have commanded the [Allied] POW camp administration. The Japanese camp commandant, Lieutenant Morimoto, thought differently though. Morimoto, otherwise known to the POWs as 'Jack Oakie', in dubious tribute to the American actor who played the role of Napolini in Charlie Chaplin's film, The Great Dictator, refused to acknowledge Fliniau, and so command remained with Major Houghton.

The Americans, around fifty in number, were given sleeping quarters in the attic where they remained until the American officers, aside from Fliniau, were moved to another camp. Fliniau then moved into the office, which he shared with Houghton for the following two years until all the [non-medical] officers were transferred to another camp in March 1945. The office was also shared with another American, Corporal Hoblitt of the United States Marine Corps, a remarkable man who spoke Japanese and served through the following two years as an interpreter and conduit between the Japanese and Allied administrations.

For the twenty or so American enlisted men who remained, sleeping in the attic was a mixed blessing. Kobe House was nicknamed the ice box for a reason – it was a brick-built warehouse, never intended to be used as accommodation, and it would have been difficult to keep the place warm, even if any serious attempt had been made. Not to mention that, regardless of the weather, the windows were left open all day whilst the working parties were out. But at night, given the heat generated by hundreds of bodies, the fourth floor was the warmest place to be, and the Americans appreciated the thermal benefits of sleeping on a platform built up into the peak of the roof. But the price paid for sleeping in the relatively warm part of the building was having to go down four flights of stairs on the frequent nighttime toilet visits that resulted from a diet based mainly on rice, which caused a noticeable increase in frequency of urination. Then, as if this wasn't bad enough, intermittent bouts of diarrhoea could turn an inconvenient walk into a frantic dash.

Denton, with what one of his friends [later] described as a 'Jimmy Cagney' persona, was the sort of person likely to gel with the Americans. Though, aside from struggling with unfamiliar accents, the Americans seemed generally to mix well with both the British and then the Australians who arrived later that year. But for Denton, music best bridged the gap, with Denton and his pals providing the entertainment, and the Americans providing the attic venue.

Working in the hospital had thrown Denton into the company of Corporal Florence, and they quickly became close friends. The two men also discovered a shared love of music and song and decided to form a musical act. Of course, other men sought release in other ways, and the handful of books that circulated were much in demand, whilst discussion and debate were invaluable too. But, for Denton and pals, music was their way to fight back against the intellectual impoverishment of being a POW, and a release from the mental stress of surviving the daily battle against disease, hunger, overwork, and casual unpredictable brutality. And in an odd way, music and entertainment had a similar psychological effect on its makers as carrying out sabotage did for some men on working parties.

When a soldier surrenders and goes into captivity the experience brings with it all sorts of emotional baggage stretching from gut-wrenching guilt to heady euphoria. In surrender is shame, humiliation, and a feeling of nigh emasculation. Joe Denton always [for the rest of his life] resented having been ordered to surrender in Hong Kong, as did many other men who felt the same and had wanted to fight on. Yet still be alive when so many others had been killed or maimed, to know that the danger was over and that one would not die was a twisted blend of angst provoking joy.

The immediacy and relief of having survived had long passed for most POWs though. The Japanese had taken away a lot more than badges and insignia from these men when they denuded them of their uniforms and dressed them in cast off Japanese Army rags. Now they were virtually slaves, beings with no rights and little perceived value, and finding ways to hit back and reassert an identity was an imperative. Making music and providing entertainment, just like sabotage, was doing something that wasn't just an obedient response to a Japanese command, was actively instigating something, no matter how humble, and being productive on their own behalf. This was all part of a process that allowed the entertainers to take back their self-respect, to reinstate their masculinity - though few, if any, would have consciously rationalised it quite this way at the time.

The benefits of creating music, song, or comedy, were obviously not confined just to the entertainers themselves, performance also had the power, for a little time at least, to lift the other POWs' out of the miseries that captivity brought. Aware of this, Florence and Denton teamed up with Private Tom Haines, Colour Sergeant Bill Poulter, and Private Charles Stanton to form a musical act. Poulter and Stanton later dropped out leaving the group to become the Harmony Three. And, to add to the variety, another group of Denton's pals - men who were to become true brothers in arms - later formed an act that they called The Mad Gang.

Nothing in POW existence was straightforward though. It might be thought that allocating time and mental energy to music wouldn't have seemed a priority to overworked, constantly hungry men. Yet oddly or ironically - or both perhaps – whilst malnutrition caused illness and disease, it also brought intellectual benefits. Presumably, the POWs' starvation rations will have taken these men into a metabolic state of ketosis as they produced ketone bodies from their rapidly diminishing reserves of body fat to use as energy in the absence of enough dietary carbohydrates. And ketosis has long been known to enhance mental performance and focus, which might explain, in part at least, the talented and creative musical and comedic output that would come from Colley, Denton, and some of the others during their time at Kobe House.

Regardless, Houghton was quick to realise that fostering morale and the will to survive was just as important as rations, and he set himself to the task of obtaining permission for concerts and in getting hold of some instruments. But, more immediately the hospital staff had their hands full dealing with the surge of illness and death that followed in the wake of the *Lisbon Maru*. So, Denton continued his medical duties under the guidance of the trained medics, including Leading Sick Berth Attendant McGreen, Petty Officer Flynn, and Corporal Florence, with Staff Sergeant Ross acting as wardmaster.

The ongoing establishment of the hospital in the latter part of October and into November was accompanied by an outbreak of diphtheria. This was almost inevitable, given the presence of already infected prisoners onboard the Lisbon Maru where the conditions had created the perfect breeding house for cross-infection and disease.

In a belated attempt to limit the spread of infection, the Japanese administration moved the [POW] officers who were billeted on the floor above the hospital to the other block. Whilst, to relieve the overcrowding, some patients were transferred to the hospital at the Stadium, from where they either died or were later returned to Kobe House. One of them was Captain Christopher Man, from the Middlesex Regiment, who was to rise to the rank of Major-General after the war. As an aside, many years after the war, Denton, now long retired and a grandfather, was attending a relative's (army) passing out parade. After the parade, whilst he was leaving, he heard a bellowed shout of 'Denton!' and turned to see Major-General Man. The two men were delighted to see each other, even so long after meeting in Kobe House hospital, or perhaps even more so because of the years, and Man invited Denton and his wife to come to visit him at his home in Pitlochry, Scotland, where he commanded the Atholl Highlanders, the Duke of Atholl's private army.

Friendship didn't readily ensue between Lance-Bombardiers and Captains [later generals] in the British Army. Of course, war and shared hardships tend to breed comradeship and respect. But illness, dependency, and the intimacy of caring, also creates its own special bonds between men: the distancing of rank and social class disappear rapidly whilst lying in a pool of your own bloody diarrhoea and calling for help.

Every day in the hospital had the potential to be different and unpredictable though, with the arrival of new patients and new challenges. Yet at the same time there were tasks like washing patients, emptying faeces buckets, and so on, which ebbed and flowed in tandem with the level of disease and injury, but remained an omnipresent drudgery in the orderlies' daily life.

Normal routines in a British military hospital followed well established patterns - wake the patients, administer medicines, breakfast, bathing, visits from doctors and surgeons, and a myriad of other tasks backed up by legions of ancillary staff and administrative resources. But Kobe House had precious little in the way of drugs, bandages, equipment, or even a doctor. So, each task just had to be worked out in the best way that the orderlies could devise.

For instance, dysentery stalked Kobe House from the day that the POWs arrived to the day that they left. Some men died of it, many survived and soldiered on. But, in the hospital, it presented the orderlies with an ongoing challenge - aside from caring for the sick men - they had to wash and reuse soiled clothing and blankets, and dispose of buckets of faeces, and so on, whilst lacking adequate washing and toilet facilities.

The hospital was on the first floor, whilst the toilets or latrines were on the ground floor. Sick, debilitated, sometimes dying men had no chance of getting from the hospital to the toilets. So, aside from the times when they would lose bowel control so violently and unexpectedly that they soiled their blankets, they were given bedpans. The bedpans would then, in turn, be emptied into pots. Then, obviously, the pots had to be carried to the latrine and then emptied out.

For many patients, the humiliation of losing control of one's bowels and having to be nursed by their comrades was eased somewhat both by ubiquity and the soldiers' humour that buoyed them up. Pain, though, was another matter, and one of the symptoms of [untreated] dysentery is violent agonising bowel cramps. In another, more humane, more modern setting, these might be treated with analgesics and anti-spasmodic medication. Lacking access to medicines, the orderlies had to just carry on as best they could. But dealing with the needs of men in pain, whilst lacking the means to help, brings the challenge of remaining calm and sympathetic whilst continuing with whatever needs to be done. It requires the outward portrayal of calm and the internal burying of stress, holding in the frustration, anger, and frantic helplessness, whilst developing the emotional detachment to enable one to carry on day after day. The orderlies learned this well enough to keep going, through like many Far East POWs, many incurred psychological debts that demanded repayment in the decades after the war.

More immediately, lifting a man off a bedpan necessitated learning the twin trick of wiping and cleaning the patient whilst at the same time trying to avoid soiling the bedding. Lacking soap, towels, toilet paper, or anything disposable, the orderlies used cold water and whatever bits of rag they could scrounge or improvise, to wipe the patient. The faecal stink, and bloody stools that tended to accompany dysentery, made the process of cleaning even more challenging for the orderlies, who of course lacked gloves. And for patients, the frequent bowel movements resulted in painful excoriated skin - a misery that might occasionally be added to by a rectal prolapse.

The bedpans were emptied into one of the pots used to store urine and faeces. Denton was only one of the orderlies, including some volunteers from the Middlesex Regiment, faced with the task of emptying these pots at intervals throughout the day (and night, if necessary). Carrying pots full of foul watery faeces, plus urine, was an unenviable task, so naturally the orderlies had to fathom out the best (or least-worst) procedure. In these situations, one school of thought is to leave the pots or buckets until they are as full as possible, the benefit being fewer trips carrying them to the disposal point. But, at Kobe House, where the pots had to be carried-down stairs to the latrine, this increased the risks of spillage which then had to be cleaned up. The alternative strategy being to empty the pots more frequently, before they were full, with less risk of spillage, but more trips up and down the stairs.

Either way, once the orderlies got the pots to the latrine, they had to walk with their feet sometimes crunching through a floor heaving with maggots from the pit latrine, which was often overflowing due to the [Japanese] administration's failure to have it emptied often enough. Then the pots had to be cleaned out with cold water, dried as best could be managed, and carried back upstairs to the hospital ready to be refilled.

Another perennial task that the orderlies shared was washing bedding and bandages. In a normal hospital soiled bedding would be sent to a specialist laundry, whilst dressings would be disposed of as clinical waste. But at Kobe House, bedding of any kind, bandages or dressings, and the few items of equipment issued to the hospital by the Japanese camp administration, had to be washed and then re-used ad infinitum.

So, soiled bedding, bandages, or whatever, had to be folded up and carried downstairs to the washing trough, taking care not to drip urine or any other waste on the floor or stairs. Aside from it causing yet more [cleaning-up] work, such 'crimes,' if detected, would prompt a bashing from a Japanese sentry. Then, best practice being to scrape off solid waste from the bedding or dressing, or whatever, before trying to wash it.

So picture, therein, Joseph Denton, former child music hall star, Hong Kong radio broadcaster, a dapper ladies' man who'd enjoyed driving around Hong Kong in his two-seater sports car, the immaculate booted and spurred Royal Artillery horseman, now dressed in cast-off Japanese Army uniform, standing next to the stinking open latrine pit, scraping smeared faeces off a blanket and flicking it from his fingers into the latrine. It wasn't quite the outcome his ambitious show-biz impresario mother had groomed him for!

Generally lacking soap or hot water, Denton and the rest of the orderlies did the best they could to get things clean. Urine washes out reasonably well, but faeces, especially the black tarred rank-smelling accompaniment to intestinal bleeding, leaves an imprint in bedding that no amount of handwashing ever removes. And getting pus or blood from bandages and dressings was an equally difficult task. But that done, the final stage was to hang everything up in the drying flat between the two blocks, collect any dry washing, and then climb back up the wooden hill ready to start again…

Meanwhile, the patients – not to mention the orderlies – needed to be fed. The belief of the Japanese administration was that hospital patients, contributing nothing to the Japanese war effort, did not deserve food at all. Grudgingly stopping short of this, they allocated half-rations both to the sick men plus the orderlies caring for them – an equally worthless and unproductive group in Japanese eyes. Losing half of what was already barely enough food to sustain life was a virtual death sentence for sick men, and a slap in the face for the volunteer orderlies already risking their own health from the cocktail of illness and infection. In recompense, the shortfall was made up by sharing from the [officially allocated] rations of the workers, soon to be leavened by smuggled contributions from outside work parties.

Diphtheria had arrived at Kobe House along with the survivors of the *Lisbon Maru* and, lacking medicines, or even a doctor's advice, the orderlies could do little more than to try to make the patients comfortable and let the disease run its course. But the lack of drugs in the hospital was not due to some sort of wartime shortage or any rationally understood reason. On the contrary, there was a storeroom in the camp with a supply of medicines, including quinine, aspirin, and sulpha [sulphonamide antibiotics] which had been brought from the Philippines by the American detachment. However, Lieutenant Morimoto, the Japanese camp commander, refused to allow the orderlies to make use of these. In fact, he'd even laughed, openly, when Lieutenant Colonel Fliniau approached him, on the orderlies' behalf, explaining that men were dying for lack of medicine.

Whether any of the drugs would have benefitted the diphtheria patients is questionable, clinically speaking. However, there is absolutely no doubt that many of the men who died of dysentery might have been saved if the orderlies had been allowed to administer the sulphonamides languishing on the storeroom shelf. In all this, though, there was nothing that Denton or anyone else in the hospital could do, instead they had to soldier-on, each frustration growing another hard scale in a thickening emotional carapace.

Diphtheria, easily spread by coughing or sneezing, eventually began to concentrate the collective mind of the Japanese camp administration whose vacillating policies predictably favoured their own safety. Consequently, some medicines began to make their way into the hospital, whether from being issued, in response to bribery, or on occasion smuggled in from outside camp. Though serum, obtained specifically for an American officer, Commander O'Brien, arrived too late to help him and he died, leaving a British officer, who consequently lived, as the serum's beneficiary – a winner in the lottery of POW life.

Unvaccinated diphtheria cases carried around a ten percent mortality given early diagnosis and treatment. The orderlies, most having left the UK prior to the vaccination programs instigated during the war years, mulled over how to deal with their situation. The symptoms of diphtheria were well known, especially to Florence and the other trained medics. Cutaneous diphtheria caused sores, red skin, and ulcers, whilst its' respiratory cousin presented with fever, chills, and a sore throat. Untreated, the disease creates a toxin that can affect the nervous system, causing paralysis and heart failure. The toxin also causes an ever-thickening coating on the throat, which makes it hard to breathe and swallow, until (in the worst cases) the patient slowly chokes to death.

The 'Strangling Angel' transmits via respiration, coughing and sneezing, or by close physical contact with bodily fluids, or even soiled bedding. So, the orderlies, themselves immune compromised by malnutrition, and lacking even the most basic equipment, such as gloves, surgical masks, or even soap, were putting themselves at risk of infection by continuing to work in the hospital.

Diphtheria though, subsumed into the general miasma of POW illness, was just one problem for the orderlies and not necessarily the worst of them. Caring for the dying, regardless of cause or manner, can be an unenviable task. But having done our best we reach for the usual time-worn bromides; 'eighty-three, he had a good innings,' 'it was his time,' and so on. What consolation can a man find though, when watching one's comrades, young men, dying from nutritional diseases whilst yards away from a well-stocked food store and the Red Cross medical supplies hoarded by the Japanese camp administration. What questions did Denton torment himself with after watching another death – should I have risked another beating by demanding medicines – should I have fought the constant hunger pains and given him my own food ration – could I have done more – the questions go on and on.

And what, for example, might best be said to the young man lying on the matting in Kobe House hospital, his throat swollen from diphtheria, weakened lungs struggling to suck in breath. Which dubious platitudes might work best - 'chin up, mate,' or perhaps, 'stick with it, you'll be okay.' Do the lies best help the fears of the dying man or calm the frantic desperation hidden inside the orderly, really, do they help at all. And whose prayers for an end to this misery are heard first, the dying man begging for release, or the orderly at the end of his emotional tether, wordlessly mouthing the words 'for God's sake man, hurry up and die!' What does such thinking do to a man - and what inadequacies do *we* offer in years to come when the guilt-memories flood back in - 'Sorry Joe, not your fault, you did your best.'

Of course, not every day was accompanied by death – though far too many were, especially in the first few months. Indeed, around one hundred men died unnecessarily during that first winter, mostly from beriberi, pneumonia, dysentery, and starvation, exacerbated by overwork and brutality. Kobe House became a place where men were tested, broken, discarded in a cruelly impersonal lottery. Yet it was also a forge, and its hospital was a crucible where every death, every beating, every unwanted indignity moulded Joseph Denton and created the man.

ESCAPE

Boredom, monotony, ennui, were the ubiquitous bane of much prisoner of war experience. In POW camps in Germany men fought back with dreams and plots about escaping. Some prisoners even transitioned dream to reality and 'got through the wire.' And a few men, usually with help from the civilian population of occupied countries, even made a home run back to England. Despite the very real dangers and difficulties in German occupied Europe, geography, some degree of shared racial homogeneity, and captors that mostly abided by the accepted accords for re-captured POWs made escape attempts feasible at least, and around 0.7 percent of POWs succeeded in getting home. In Japan, the situation was somewhat different.

Denton, like every POW at Kobe House, yearned for an end to his incarceration. To be sure, no man long behind bars can avoid thoughts of *what if*. And the POWs were aware that there had been some successful escapes from Hong Kong in the early days after the Christmas Day surrender, success facilitated to some extent by the proximity of a Chinese civilian populace who deeply hated their Imperial Japanese Army occupiers. But the situation in Japan was different, it was an island impractically distanced from the nearest allied or neutral territory, where Caucasians stood out in stark contrast to a hostile indigenous populace. Escapes there, and there were a few attempts, all ended quickly, and badly.

Regardless of practicality, there were other reasons behind the Allied military code which instructed every POW to attempt to escape. Escape attempts in Germany and occupied Europe, even when unsuccessful, aided the Allied war effort by tying down and diverting large numbers of enemy military and civil resources. So, why then, one might ask, didn't Denton do his bit and have stab at it.

Well one man in the Kobe and Osaka area did try to escape, and the results were painfully instructive to the POW body collective. Kobe House was part of the Osaka POW camp administration, itself under the command of Colonel Murata, who had made his presence felt in the face slapping parade that Denton had avoided shortly after arriving at Kobe House. And if there was any doubt about Murata's feelings about escape attempts, he soon made them crystal clear by his response to Private Tyler's attempt.

Private Everett Tyler, an American soldier imprisoned at a nearby camp, decided (for reasons which must forever remain his own) to try to escape. Given the virtual impossibility of travelling, or even hiding, Japanese Army security was often kept at a level that it made it possible for POWs to evade immediate captivity and get out of a camp. This is what Tyler did but, ragged, hungry, emaciated, and generally sticking out like a Caucasian sore thumb amongst the Japanese civilian population, he was recaptured a few hours later.

Tyler was returned to his camp and taken into the guardroom, near the camp entrance. Details thenceforth vary depending on witness recall and the who did what blame shifting when, some years later, the perpetrators were brought to account. But the essence of it is that Tyler was ordered to stand to attention, and then the beating began with the mandatory bout of face slapping. Making victims stand to attention was a norm, it mirrored such procedure within the Japanese Army, and POWs knew that failure to comply would invariably worsen the level of punishment meted out. So, Tyler stood to attention and then some of the guards (and possibly some civilians) took wooden bars from a door and the punishment began. How long this first beating lasted is a matter for conjecture now, but it lasted long enough for Tyler's screams to be heard by other POWs from outside the building.

Numerous beatings, violence of differing means, such as being hammered by bamboo poles thrust through his cell window, continued at intervals over the next couple of days. In the meantime, Colonel Murata was informed of Tyler's escape attempt and subsequent re-capture. As the officer commanding all Kobe and Osaka POW camps, Murata was responsible for the secure incarceration of the POWs. But, according to the Geneva conventions, he was also responsible for their welfare and safety.

It bears reiteration that when viewed from the situational ethics of Japanese military belief, the POWs were considered both to have forfeited the right to life and to now owe absolute unquestioning obedience to Japanese military law and discipline. So, from Murata's blinkered perspective, Tyler had therein committed a capital offence. In military terms, Tyler's escape, albeit short lived, was perceived personally by Murata as a professional dishonour that caused him to lose face. Hence Murata, clearly enraged, ordered Tyler to be 'disposed of.'

On Tyler's final day in the guardhouse POW witnesses observed him trying to stand to attention, vomiting blood whilst he was being beaten again. Such were the fine details of Private Tyler's experiences, the obiter dicta to a lesson, one of a series of lessons really, that filtered through to (and were not lost on) his contemporaries.

Tyler was finally sent to the POW hospital at Ichioka Stadium. He was bruised, bleeding, and only semi-conscious during the journey after Lieutenant Shoichi Nosu gave him an injection of ether. Nosu was a Japanese Army doctor, and the chief medical administrator of all the POW camps in the Osaka area, including Kobe House and Ichioka POW hospital (where [some] sick POWs from Kobe House were sent to on occasion).

Lieutenant Nosu, and a Japanese Army medical orderly, Lance-Corporal Masaichi Toyama, travelled with Tyler in the back of the lorry. Tyler watched, eyes open, and partly conscious as Nosu gave him more injections, probably morphine. This failed to kill Tyler, so Toyama held an ether-soaked gauze over his mouth for around twenty minutes. It's not entirely clear whether Private Tyler eventually died as a result of the ether, the beatings, or the injections, or perhaps their combination. Nor is it clear whether he was still even partially conscious upon arrival. What is certain though, is that Colonel Murata was at the hospital awaiting Tyler's arrival. After Tyler was unloaded from the lorry Murata stood and watched for an hour or so until Tyler was dead. Finally, satisfied, after finally getting to gaze on Tyler's corpse, Murata departed, 'face' regained.

Such vignettes might seem a little strained viewed through contemporary mores. The writer strives for effect, perhaps. Maybe the portrayal of the health professionals, Doctor Nosu, or Medical Orderly Toyama, stretches twenty-first century credulity. Should there be any doubt or scepticism though, further proofs readily present themselves. For example, Murata later ordered two other POWs to be executed at the POW hospital. Then, a compliant Doctor Nosu took the two men, hooded and bound, after the usual beatings and abuse and murdered them with cyanide injections. The irony, such as it is, is not that these incidents need exaggeration or literary license. On the contrary, such things were commonplace in the Japanese Army's prison camps. So then, if one was able to ask Lance Bombardier Joseph Denton why he didn't carry out his duty to attempt an escape from Japanese captivity, he might well sum it up by answering, 'Everett Tyler.'

With physical escape being firmly off the menu, Denton's thoughts returned, often, to music. But, aside from concerns over the likely response of the Japanese camp administration, not having musical instruments limited the potential for concerts or anything more formal than occasional a cappella entertainments. At least though the work in the hospital was easing up, after the hectic first months with many of the first rush of patients either recovered, transferred, or dead. But the lack of a doctor was a continuing concern to all the medical orderlies.

The hospital's governance was always subject to the direction of a Japanese Army medical orderly. These men were often brutal and incompetent, and generally more interested in stealing the already meagre medical supplies than in the welfare of the patients. On occasion they would prescribe treatment, and administer drugs, over-riding the POW medics (and later the POW doctors), and prisoners sometimes died as a result of their interventions. Not all of them fitted the stereotype though, a few were decent men who did their best. But, even these had little to contribute in the way of useful medical knowledge. Their training, in the Japanese Army, was generally limited to some very basic nursing, and tasks such as cleaning and bandaging wounds and acting as stretcher bearers.

The Japanese Army medical soldiers at Kobe House, regardless of individual competence, shouldered a primary duty – which was *not* the welfare of the sick and dying. Their task was to maintain the supply of a certain number of men for work each day regardless of the general health of the prisoners, and to do this they had to keep the total number of hospitalised POWs as low as possible. In the summer of 1943 this was formally codified by Lieutenant Morimoto, the Japanese camp commandant, who ordered that no more than fifteen sick POWs could remain in camp. So, whenever necessary they would send sick men out to work and even punish the POW orderlies for failing to keep the number of sick men down.

Denton spent around two and a half years living and working in the hospital at Kobe House, though many of the other volunteer orderlies were gradually re-allocated to outside work parties as the hospital in-patient numbers fell. Of course, the character of the Japanese Army medics, who had de facto power of life or death over the POWs, mattered to everyone. But for Denton, living and working closely with them for so long, understanding and accommodating their lethal idiosyncrasies was a matter of personal survival.

The Japanese orderlies would hold a sick parade to choose the fifteen men who were to be allowed to remain hospitalised on any given day. Not surprisingly, there were often far more than fifteen sick men, sixty or seventy not being unusual. So, the [Japanese Army] orderlies devised their own selection procedures. One of them, Okasaki, liked to parade the sick men and march them up and down the yard outside shouting drill orders in Japanese. Often, prisoners would collapse unconscious during the selection until at some stage, Okasaki would select fifteen. The remaining sick men, a few carried on another man's back, many others supported and half-carried by friends, were sent out with the work parties. Then, at the end of the day, they would be carried back to camp by men who were themselves tired, weakened, and debilitated.

The Japanese Army medical orderlies came and went over the following two years, each wielding their own foibles. One of these orderlies stole, and sold, some of the American Red Cross medical supplies that arrived in 1944, and liberally dosed himself with the limited supply of the Vitamin Pills intended for POWs suffering from avitaminosis. Another Japanese Army medic, who always wore a pair of spectacles, was known to Denton and the other orderlies as The Four-Eyed Bastard. 'Four-Eyes' took an especial interest in the frequent cases of dysentery that came into the hospital and put these patients under his direct supervision. His own unique brand of medical treatment then was to order that these already malnourished men should be starved. This was so he could take their tiny mid-day ration of a small bread roll for himself, having first ordered one of the volunteer medical orderlies to take the bread to the camp kitchen to be toasted.

In an odd twist to the tale, Four-Eyes, who had a taste for sweet things, liked to spread his toast with some of the hospital's tiny store of cough linctus. It was the final straw and eventually he was reported to the Japanese camp sergeant major [Morita]. Complaining about the criminal actions of any of the Japanese Army guards was a risky affair, that, in most camps, could lead to violent reprisals. However, in a piece of restorative justice that wasn't lost on the POWs, the camp sergeant major (who would later earn something of a reputation for fair play), personally gave Four-Eyes the beating he thoroughly deserved before ensuring him transferred to another camp.

On the 9th March 1943, the camp was visited by Doctor Pescelli, a representative of the International Red Cross. In anticipation, the Japanese Army administration filled the stores and kitchens with food and supplies though these were withdrawn again immediately after the representative's departure. Regrettably, the undertone of violence and intimidation during such visits precluded much in the sense of meaningful complaint as Allied officers and camp administrators were aware that frankness would likely later result in repercussions. In fact, even visiting officials, protected by neutral status, reportedly seemed conscious and wary of their own safety.

Just before Pescelli arrived the camp was cleared of most of the POWs, who were moved across the road to a sports field, leaving only the POW admin staff and the orderlies and patients in the hospital. Pescelli talked with members of the camp administration, including Major Houghton, and Corporal Hoblitt, the American interpreter. Houghton was guarded in his comments, aiming to allow Pescelli to read between the lines, a policy for which he later drew flak from some of his fellow officers. Then

Pescelli visited the hospital and met the medical orderlies, including Denton. As both regular soldiers and POWs experienced in the realities of prison life, the orderlies knew better than to make direct complaint themselves. Like Houghton, they said little, instead allowing the evidence to speak for itself.

Private Joseph Duff had died the evening before the Red Cross visit, from cardiac beriberi. And as he arrived next morning, Pescelli may have seen Duff's corpse, stuffed into a half-barrel, at the usual collection point next to the camp entrance. Pescelli may also have walked past the corpse of Private John Huggett, another hospital patient, who died a few hours after Duff, from acute pneumonia. Whilst amongst the living patients presented for inspection later in the day, Private Robert Tyrer, another pneumonia patient, lay weakened by starvation and malnutrition, labouring for breath, clearly with only a few hours of life left to him. Doctor Pescelli observed this scene, understanding made obvious in his expression, whilst Denton, his pal Florence, indeed all the orderlies, stood there amongst the mute and dying evidence that spoke volumes on their behalf.

INTERESTING TIMES

The medical orderlies might well have agreed with the assertion that June 1943 nicely fitted the apocryphal curse of 'interesting times.' The rates of illness had slowed down, with only one-man, Corporal Andrew Chalmers, leaving the hospital in a wooden barrel that month. And wisdom, medically speaking, arrived on June 8th in the shape of Australian doctor, Captain Clive Boyce. Whilst foolishness, to the point of criminal stupidity, arrived two days later in the person of Japanese doctor, Lieutenant Kunio Miyatake.

Doctor Boyce and around two-hundred-and-fifty other Australian officers and other ranks arrived in Japan as part of J Force – a detachment sent out from a prison camp in Singapore. They'd been told that they were going to a rest camp with light work and pleasant convalescence facilities for the numerous sick men amongst them. No doubt they'd listened to this with a cynical ear – though many of them must have at least hoped for something better than where they'd come from. If so, they were abruptly disillusioned upon arrival at Kobe House.

The Australians were welcomed by Colonel Murata, who gave them the usual spiel about how they were all criminals who were only allowed to live due to the kindness of the Emperor and how they must work hard and conform to all the rules and regulations of the Imperial Japanese Army and so on. Unimpressed, they proceeded onto the next stage which was being taught by Japanese Army guards how to count, do parade drill, and understand work orders in Japanese, the learning process being reinforced with bamboo sticks.

Some days later, the welcome ceremonies complete, the Australian soldiers were sent out on work details whilst Captain Boyce, being a doctor, was allocated to the camp hospital. Aside from having earlier been promised medicines, vitamins, good food, and light work for the party of convalescents that Boyce arrived with, he'd also been expecting to arrive at an already well established six-hundred bed hospital. The previous couple of days of drill and beatings had no doubt prepared the way for a little disappointment. However, when he finally walked into the tiny crowded ill-equipped hospital room, it's safe to say that he would have been a little less than impressed.

Boyce had brought medical orderlies with him, though only two of them, Private John Byrnes and Private Reginald Kavanagh, were permitted to join the establishment of the hospital. Boyce was unhappy with these curbs on his powers to decide the hospital staffing arrangements. Indeed, Doctor Boyce was unenthused by most everything at Kobe House. The POW's daily ration, at that time, was three tiny bowls of poor-quality rice, seasoned with three equally small bowls of vegetables. This, in Boyce's opinion, was already barely enough to sustain life, and to make matters worse, Boyce was appalled to discover that, like Denton and the other medics, [officially] he would only receive half that amount.

Boyce made frequent representation to both Fliniau and Houghton about medicines being held back by the Japanese administration. To their credit, they in turn, protested to the Japanese camp commandant. In this, as in other issues that had to be put to the Japanese administration, there were differences of opinion regarding the most effective way forward. Houghton favoured a softer diplomatic approach, and in the long term it proved to be the better tactic. For instance, most of the POWs who wore spectacles had lost them whilst escaping from the sinking *Lisbon Maru*. So, Houghton, choosing his times with care, quietly, respectfully, and repeatedly lobbied the Japanese camp administration on the matter. And, a few months later, they conceded and issued a supply of glasses to the POWS.

Time, though, often worked against the POWs - some matters by their nature demanded immediacy. When a man was dying for lack of a medicine, patience was a hard virtue to deploy. Understandably, Fliniau, and some of the younger officers might, on occasion, have preferred a somewhat stronger tack. Whilst Boyce, whose trust and support for the (mainly British) administration was somewhat qualified, urged outright confrontation.

On this, and sometimes on other issues, positional nuance also strained relations between Boyce and the hospital orderlies. These men had spent time trying to cultivate whatever degree of improved working relationship was possible given the violent caprice of the Japanese soldiers involved. Essentially, Denton's view was that it was smarter to swallow one's pride and feign interest and respect if it offered the opportunity to defuse violence or divert [Japanese] attention from interfering with the patients and the running of the hospital.

When a Japanese soldier or medical orderly walked into the hospital, they had absolute carte blanche, with little or no control or direction from the camp commandant, aside from the inviolable ruling that the number of patients had to be kept low regardless of the actual health of the prisoners. These Japanese medics had little formal education, and very limited medical knowledge. They were also instilled with hatred and contempt for POWs and indoctrinated to see a culture of violence and unquestioning obedience to authority – in this case, theirs – as a norm. Essentially, to a greater or lesser extent, each one was a walking powder keg and the POW orderlies made the decision to tread softly and avoid lighting the fuse.

It's easy now, of course, from the standpoint of western liberal culture and education to cognise the Japanese Army guards themselves, their actions, through one's own innate moral prism and sit in accordant judgement. Though this, of course, is pretty much what the guards did with the POWs, albeit viewed through a very different lens. Anyway, the POW orderlies could read their captors for signs, whether of weakness or humanity, and respond accordingly. Many of the guards had families, a subject that most of them enjoyed talking about - especially their children. They would, on occasion, come into the hospital either to practice their limited English or show off photographs of their spouse or children. The orderlies would, in response, make admiring noises and exchange [sometime truthful] accounts of their own baby making prowess – something the Japanese guards admired on a 'the more the better' principle. This, however, doesn't mean that any of the orderlies genuinely wanted to ooh and ah over happy-snaps of some guard's progeny. The underlying reality to Denton was that both guards and their accompanying photographs were as welcome in the hospital as a plague of boils.

But whether the orderlies were recognising a sign of shared humanity, or cleverly manipulating an enemy's weakness, was of little import at the time. What did matter, for the orderlies, was that a pleased guard was more likely to act decently, and far less likely to demonstrate his curative skills upon the defenceless patients with his boots. Boyce, however, looked upon the orderlies' attempts to placate the guards with disdain. He continued to feel strongly that confrontation brought better results. And it was a perfectly valid point of view, as on some occasions it might - though, arguably, it more often resulted in the opposite. Regardless of Boyce's feelings on this issue though, the orderlies continued to favour the more subtle approach.

Subtlety was also the way that Houghton, as the British [camp] commander, continued to make small victories and improvements, in a gradual process of taking back management [from the Japanese administration] of as many internal administrative tasks as he could. For instance, he regained control of the allocation of men to jobs and working parties: one benefit of this being that men could be assigned to, or kept from, certain work parties, so that the sicker men could be sent to the relatively lighter jobs.

Of course, Denton had little influence in anything beyond his own immediate actions. Nor did he have any say in the ongoing command dilemma between the policies of confrontation or negotiation. But, like everyone else, Denton knew one thing for sure – responses were unpredictable and, either way, whatever they did had the potential to backfire. For instance, Colonel Fliniau wrote a letter to Lieutenant Morimoto requesting additional food for [all] the POWs. This was a most reasonable request given that, especially in the first year or so of the camp's existence, men were starving whilst at the same time there were adequate supplies of food in the camp stores. In response, nothing bad happened to the letter's author, though neither did any extra rations get issued to the prisoners. Another time Fliniau protested to Morimoto about the fact that POWs were dying for lack of the vitamins and medicines which were sitting, unissued, in the stores. Morimoto's reaction, on this occasion, was to stand and laugh at Fliniau.

Then, not to be outdone, the British officers made a joint written complaint to Morimoto protesting about the withholding of medical supplies, inadequate clothing, starvation level rations, and the general mistreatment of the soldiers under their [very nominal] command. Morimoto was furious, he ordered the officers to muster outside the guardroom and left them there standing rigidly to attention for hours. Of course, they were well used to military drill. However, all parade drill was now carried out according to Japanese Army regulations, and the act of standing to attention was far more physically demanding than they were used to. Quite literally, even the act of moving one's eyeballs slightly, if noticed by the guards overseeing them, could result in an immediate and savage beating. Eventually Lieutenant Morimoto came and addressed them. He called them troublemakers, before going on to make it clear that any further protest would result in harsh reprisals. And, of course, they had been in Japanese custody long enough now to understand the truth of such a warning.

Denton was equally aware of the dangers of interacting with Japanese Army personnel, especially the new arrival - Miyatake. Doctor Miyatake, who'd arrived at Kobe House just after Boyce, would soon become known to the POWs as the 'Mad Doctor.' Miyatake had a special liking for beating men with his sword scabbard, a process that the POWs nicknamed being knighted, whilst another of his favoured pastimes was flogging men with the buckle end of his belt. In fact, one of Denton's friends and a member of the Mad Gang, Private James McDougall, soon found himself on the receiving end of Miyatake's rage.

Miyatake conducted an inspected of the sleeping quarters and he found two lead pencils. It was against camp regulations for ORs to be in possession of a pencil and so Miyatake, easily enraged, demanded to know who owned them. None of the assembled soldiers volunteered an answer and Miyatake grew even more angry. Being a Sunday (rest day) the building was full of soldiers, all stood to attention in silence in front of Miyatake, with the situation on the verge of blowing up. Whether or not the pencils belonged to McDougall isn't clear, but to save the situation he stepped forward and admitted ownership. In response, Miyatake kicked McDougall in the stomach and he fell backwards onto the sleeping platform. Miyatake kept kicking McDougall, and hitting him with a sword scabbard, until he stood up again. After this the punishment was continued for another ten or fifteen minutes with more sword blows and repeated kicks in the stomach, and then McDougall was sent to stand to attention outside the guardroom for the rest of the day before the orderlies were eventually allowed to attend to his wounds.

Miyatake, thoroughly capricious, was one of those Japanese soldiers who loved to show his family photographs to the medics. Whilst Boyce and the two Australian orderlies distanced themselves, the Irish and British orderlies, Denton, Florence, Ross, and the others, made admiring noises and tried to avoid provoking Miyatake. It's safe to say though, given Miyatake's general conduct, which was extreme even by Japanese Army standards, that during such interactions Joe Denton would much rather have stuffed the photographs down the Miyatake's throat, accompanied by their proud owner's dentition.

Photographs aside, it was inevitable that Boyce and Miyatake would lock horns over most every issue or procedure, medical supplies being just one of them. Miyatake had control of the medical stores, aided by a Japanese soldier whose duty it was to collect the supplies from the storeroom. Boyce had to make his supply requests via this soldier, or Houghton's office. But, regardless of the request channel, the response was often that Miyatake, for no reason aside from sadistic whim, would refuse to allow medicines to be issued and sometimes men died who might well have lived had they been allowed treatment.

Prior to Miyatake's arrival, there were usually two Tenkos [roll call] each day. In the summer the first Tenko was at 5 a.m. and in the winter it would be at 6 a.m., whilst the evening roll call was held at 8 p.m. Doctor Miyatake, however, in addition to his medical duties also got rostered as orderly officer [as part of the Japanese camp administration] at least once a week. Seemingly the good doctor disliked this duty, so he took the opportunity to take out his frustrations on the POWs by parading them two or three times a night for roll calls. And in this, and much else besides, Miyatake made no secret of his dislike of POWs in general, and the Australians in particular.

Private Arthur 'Tibby' Jeynes, one of the Australian soldiers who arrived along with Boyce, fell afoul of Miyatake one evening when he was orderly officer. Miyatake walked into the [Australian soldiers'] sleeping quarters and saw that Jeynes had a cigarette. It was after the evening Tenko, and smoking wasn't allowed at this time. However, according to numerous witnesses, Jeynes' cigarette wasn't lit, it was merely in his possession. This was enough for Miyatake though, and, ignoring Jeynes' explanation, he ordered two guards to take him to the guardroom.

Miyatake arrived shortly afterwards to carry out the beating. At the same time a British POW, Private Lipscome, in the process of passing by on the way back to his quarters, failed to bow in a sufficiently respectful manner. So Miyatake thrashed him and then kicked him when he collapsed to the floor. But his real ire was reserved for Jeynes.

Gripping his thick leather army officer's belt with two hands, to get the maximum force behind his blows, Miyatake repeatedly struck Jeynes across the lower face. Boyce, and possibly some of the orderlies, witnessed part of the beating. Whilst Denton and the others counted the thumps as the belt smacked into Jeynes' face - the noise clearly audible, even at a distance - seventy-three blows in total.

Jeynes stood there for around an hour, being kicked back up on his feet each time he collapsed, his face slowly being beaten into a bloody mess. The orderlies' thoughts as they listened to the punishment are not too difficult to deduce – primarily sympathy, of course. But maybe guilt and frustration too, wanting to intervene but knowing that to do so would be nigh suicidal - plus, the inevitable silent axiom, 'thank God, it isn't *me*.'

August 12 [1943] started off pretty much like any other day.

Denton took his rations in the hospital, as usual. The main body of the POWs had their breakfast, such as it was, paraded, and were then marched off in their gangs to the various places of work. One of these contingents, mainly Australian, was taken to Kobe docks, where they had been working for the previous three weeks, unloading coal into barges from a Japanese ship moored in the harbour.

Working on these barges was unpopular, because there was no opportunity to pilfer food. Shovelling coal is also hard labour too, at the best of times, even for fit, strong, well fed men. The POWs though, were thin, diseased, and hungry. And to make matters worse, they were perpetually tired, not least due to the actions of Lieutenant Miyatake, who was making them get up two or three times a night for roll call.

There's little doubt that sleep deprivation contributes to industrial accidents and, in this case, it likely precipitated the demise of Private Walter Hall. Hall, an Australian infantryman, better known as 'Legs' to his mates, was having a break from shovelling coal and was on deck unhooking the coal nets after they had been winched out of the ship's hold. Later that day, a little after two p.m., whether through his own fatigue and inattention, or a mistake by the winchman, Hall was hit by a coal net and fell into the barge. Other POWs scrambled across and found him unconscious with a head injury. They took him up onto the deck and the ship's crew hoisted a distress signal, seeking medical aid. A nearby German ship sent a boat, but the Japanese guards, ever suspicious of their Axis allies, refused to allow them to help, and Hall lay there until a launch was sent out from Kobe docks by the Japanese shipping company.

Once ashore, in Kobe, Hall was taken to a civilian hospital where his treatment consisted of being splashed with iodine. Then he was carried back to Kobe House, on a stretcher, by some POWs. They brought Hall, still unconscious, blackened from head to toe, and his face a mass of coagulated blood and coal dust, up to the camp hospital at around five p.m. The Australian doctor, at least two British trained medics, and some volunteer orderlies, including Denton, were stood waiting. But, instead of receiving medical aid, this is where Hall's troubles really began.

A few minutes later Miyatake walked in. He ordered Boyce and the orderlies not to touch Hall. Disobeying a direct order from Miyatake, especially to his face, was unthinkable. So, they stood there, frustrated and powerless, whilst Miyatake gazed dispassionately at Hall's unconscious body. It's a struggle here to imagine what was going through this so-called doctor's mind, though it was unlikely to be anything that would have resonated too well with Hippocrates. Regardless, after around five minutes, Miyatake stalked off – his order [that Hall should not be touched] still extant.

Miyatake had not said when he would return, nor even if he would return at all - though it was inevitable at some stage. So, the dilemma was how long should they wait, before taking the risk of attending to Hall, who was still lying there in front of them. And if they did decide to treat him, how much treatment was it safe [for *them*] to give – could they attend to any of Hall's injuries without it being apparent later.

Even being caught examining Hall, the patient, might now be construed as disobeying an order. Their status as prisoners of war, the Geneva Conventions, meant little. The POWs had long been told, emphatically, that they were subject to Japanese Army military laws and punishments, as if they were Japanese soldiers. They knew then, that disobeying Miyatake's direct order would likely provoke violence, that *could*, if Miyatake chose, be terminal. So, instead, should they seek out Miyatake and request his permission to attend to Hall. And whilst they debated, Private Hall lay in front of them, unconscious, dying perhaps for want of medical care.

Boyce, and the orderlies, waited for the remainder of the evening and throughout the night, painfully aware that they had a medical duty of care for Hall and that he might well die without their attention. The following day came still without a return visit from Miyatake. So, Boyce and the orderlies made the decision to begin treating Hall. The orderlies began by cleaning the coal dust off his face and head, and then Boyce dressed his wound and examined him for other injuries. Beyond this, given the limited medical facilities, and a situation complicated by Miyatake's orders, there was little that they could do except monitor Hall as he lay in the hospital, still unconscious, during the rest of the day and throughout the night.

Finally, on the 15th August, a little after 8.30 in the evening, Miyatake walked back into the hospital. Denton and the other orderlies on duty stood to attention and then bowed. Miyatake walked over to Private Hall, who lay, quite still, on the sleeping platform. Clearly enraged, he shouted an order to Hall, in Japanese, to stand to attention. Hall though, mercifully unaware of anything, moved not an inch.

Private Hall remained unconscious, so Miyatake, practicing his own unique brand of medicine, kicked him in the stomach. One can imagine the orderlies' bitter feelings of anger and frustration, watching as Miyatake's kicks progressed further up Hall's body. Then, unable to rouse Hall with his boot, Miyatake gave him a final kick in the chest then turned and walked out of the hospital. Less than two hours later, Private Hall died: he was twenty-one years old.

In an ironic twist, just before Hall's accident two brave officers had written a letter to Morimoto, the Camp Commandant, seeking Miyatake's dismissal - and the letter had been taken seriously and was scheduled to be acted upon. The letter's authors had cleverly framed their complaint in a way that *appeared* to be evincing concern about harm to the Japanese war effort. Major William 'Zaz' Pitt, of the [British] Royal Artillery, and Major Ronald Campbell, the officer commanding the Australian troops, complained that Miyatake's punitive night-time Tenkos were stopping the prisoners from getting any sleep. They avoided any complaint directed at injustice or unenforceable prisoner's rights. Instead, they emphasised that an ongoing disturbance and lack of sleep would result in tired men – with a concomitant negative effect upon their productive capacity within the Japanese war industry.

Around eleven days later, on 31st August, to the widespread but guarded pleasure of the POWs, the Mad Doctor was transferred to Osaka main camp. Bad news, of course, to the many other *Lisbon Maru* survivors at that camp who now had to suffer his excesses. But for Denton and Florence, and everyone else in the hospital, it was a red-letter day and a sign perhaps of some hope for the future. Hope, of course, being an emotion that POWs innately touched with a wary grip – unlike its cousin, the will to survive, which burned deeply and fiercely in most of Kobe House's inmates, and not least in Denton. And one expression of this burgeoning brush with optimism, that came instinctively to Florence, Denton, and some other Kobe House pals, like Ramp Bowen, was a resurgent focus on concerts and entertainment.

Houghton, conscious of the importance of retaining some sort of normality, and a few simple pleasures, in the POWs' lives, had asked the Japanese administration for permission to hold lectures, concerts, and entertainments, soon after their arrival at Kobe House. The initial response had been unpromising and platitudinous comments that war was a serious business, the POWs would be too busy working, and that the Emperor had forbidden entertainments anyway.

Nonetheless, in response to quiet persistence, the POWs were issued with some musical instruments to be used for concerts on Sundays. Whilst getting a few instruments was hugely welcomed, formal permission still had to be sought to make use of them and so Houghton requested [Japanese] approval to start an orchestra. It's a measure of the byzantine bureaucracy that governed every aspect of life that it took over a year before permission was finally granted to buy a few more instruments (at the prisoners' expense) and then form an orchestra under the leadership of Sergeant Jeffree, the former band-sergeant of the Middlesex Regiment.

Initially, permission was given to practice on Saturday evenings and then perform on Sundays. This marked the start of a slow easing process as the year progressed with more and more entertainment being allowed, including broadcasting twice a week on the camp PA system in the evenings. And this liberalisation was boosted by help from an unexpected quarter, the arrival of Hiroyuki Morita in October 1943.

Strictly speaking Morita was returning, having been at Kobe House previously when the Lisbon Maru survivors first arrived, before then being sent for duties to other camps a few weeks later. But he was back now, in the substantive rank of sergeant, to take up the post of camp sergeant major. He was still a young man, slim and a little taller than some of his contemporaries. He arrived, proud and commanding, a non-commissioned officer in the victorious Imperial Japanese Army, three stars on his collar and sword swinging by his side. But, to clarify, he was a sergeant acting in the position of sergeant-major for a specific period [the distinction would be meaningful much later when made in his defence against accusations of war crimes].

Like everyone else, Denton viewed Morita with the cynically jaundiced eye of experience. But Morita would prove to be something of an ally in the fight for survival and the two men would later part company, if not exactly friends, then at least no longer enemies. More immediately though, Denton, like most every POW, pondered the million-dollar questions - what sort of man was Morita, how would he exercise power, and how might they best deal with him.

The POWs analysed guards with all the care and attention of a racecourse tipster, which was not surprising given that on occasion in their dealings with the administration they could be betting their lives on the outcome. So, rumours, stories, and information, circulated between the camps in the Osaka area, and rumoured oddities about Morita's conduct may well have accompanied his arrival. Lieutenant Morimoto was the commander of both Kobe House and the small camp at Kawasaki, where Morita had just come from. But he had left the day to day running of the Kawasaki camp to Morita. And it's noticeable that under Morita's tenure the death rate fell well below the average for Japanese POW camps. So much so that on at least one occasion Morimoto had evidenced his displeasure with Morita's management style by beating him, and eventually he removed Morita from his post.

Japanese soldiers, of all ranks, beat and physically punished their subordinates as a commonplace disciplinary measure. Indeed, it was such an organisational norm, that they often found it hard to comprehend why POWs considered it to be an abuse when done to them. The point in this instance, though, is not the fact that Morita was punished per se, but that he was punished for being too lenient in his treatment of the POWs.

It would be specious to eulogise Morita for *not* being excessively brutal or for not stealing Kobe House's POWs' food and medicines. One might expect such standards, now, as a matter of course. But Morita was functioning in a very different realm where hierarchy and loyalty were everything, and violence and even criminality were organisational norms. Yet Morita still managed to retain some sense of justice and humanity, some sense of fair play. He would still physically punish prisoners for breaking rules, but in Denton's opinion his punishments were at least controlled and, by Japanese Army standards, proportionate.

A reduction in brutality was of course hugely welcomed. But Morita also clearly loved music and entertainment – a common bond that would be made use of by the band of talented musicians and entertainers at Kobe House. Of course, men at Kobe House still starved, slaved, suffered pain, stressed, and stopped often to listen for the rattle of the carriage wheels. Nonetheless, for Joe Denton, in a life of little hope and limited optimism, getting rid of the Mad Doctor and gaining permission to make music and give concerts felt like a blessing.

Denton's pal, Maher, neither medically nor musically inclined himself, continued working on the docks and various factories. And no doubt Maher took advantage of the chance to grab a few pilfered rations now and then, as well as appreciating a change of scene from the claustrophobic camp. Working outside was no sinecure though, and whilst some Japanese workers and foremen were reasonable enough there were others who treated the POWs like dogs. In this, as in much else, the POWs had little choice but to take whatever grief was dished out. But every man has a breaking point, and one of the POWs was pushed just too far on one occasion and he challenged the Japanese worker to a fight.

The [civilian] worker accepted, perhaps overconfident because of the generally debilitated physical condition of most POWs, or because of a fear of losing 'face' by refusing a challenge from a despised Gaijin. What he didn't know though, was that the Kobe House POWs included some outstanding boxers, this soldier being one of them. Not to put too fine a point on it, he gave the Japanese workman a real hammering – news of which soon spread amongst the POWs when the work parties returned to camp later that day.

Both Denton and Maher were also boxers, Denton being a pretty good one himself. Though ironically, the only man who ever put him on his back was his pal Maher who, according to Denton, got in a lucky punch one time during a bout in Hong Kong. Anyhow, along with the rest of the prisoners, they expected to see the soldier get punished for hitting the Japanese civilian – and indeed he was. He was put in a cell for some days, but aside from that treated well. And the Japanese guards, who didn't care too much for civilians anyway, admired him for winning in a fair fight and brought him extra rations whilst he was locked up.

NEW BROOMS

Robert Wilson, a young Irish doctor, arrived at Kobe House early in January [1944]. He'd been commissioned into the RAF, as a Flight Lieutenant, in April 1941, not long after graduating from medical school and subsequently sent to the Far East before finally being captured in Java. Wilson's move to Kobe House coincided with the issue of some [American] Red Cross medical supplies, a significant factor in the markedly decreasing camp death rate from this period onwards. And Boyce, understandably tired, was initially pleased to see another doctor too and glad of some backup and support. Boyce also liked to get out on working parties, now and then. And having another doctor in camp, to share the load, made this a little easier.

The medical orderlies also welcomed a new face if for no other reason that they were hungry for news of the outside world and the progress of the war. Though Wilson, like most new arrivals, was in no position to provide real insight. But he was young and affable, and seemed to have something of a knack for dealing with the Japanese. And Houghton, the British camp leader, was impressed with Wilson's success in wrestling some of the decision-making process from the Japanese medic in the choice of which POWs were unfit to go out to work.

Wilson - only a year older than Denton - soon became popular with the orderlies, especially Flynn and McGreen, the two Irish medics. Some of the men working outside camp also took a shine to their new doctor, and Wilson received gifts of food from the work parties which he shared with his fellow countrymen in the hospital. But few things carry more import than the topic of food to men constantly teetering on the edge of starvation in a prison camp. And not surprisingly, the flash point for food related arguments was [some] mealtimes when Boyce's resentment boiled over and the two doctors, Wilson and Boyce, argued over food allocation. It seems though that Boyce's disdain for Wilson, the junior of the two doctors, went deeper than straightforward disagreement over the equitable division of smuggled food and included professional reasons. Regardless, Denton, as part of a tight-knit team of orderlies who'd learned to work together, tried to distance himself from the spats between Wilson and Boyce.

Discord and resentments cropped up at other times too, whether between individuals or between the differing nationalities. But given the psychological powder keg of incarceration, and the lingering guilts and blamings that came with capitulation in war, perhaps some level of dissension was almost inevitable. Most of the men at Kobe House were British, Australian, and then American, added to by a small but eclectic mix of nationalities from Chinese to Maltese: Band of Brothers mythologising would have us see them all as souls united in defiant opposition to their gaolers, the reality though was a little more flawed and a lot more human.

Human frailty notwithstanding, 1944 saw a rapidly declining death rate. Whilst the Japanese camp administration was also increasingly amenable to musical entertainment, and the number of concerts increased substantially. So, with far fewer deaths and a relative lessening in the rate and severity of illnesses, the medics had a little more time for the benefit both of themselves and their remaining patients.

Singing and light-hearted comedy routines, were something that both Denton and Florence excelled in. And, as medics in the camp hospital, they were well placed to stage impromptu light entertainment for the patients, some relief from their realities, some laughter and happiness. Obviously, the patients couldn't leave camp in a literal physical sense, but emotionally and spiritually they could escape for a little while at least. And for Denton and Florence, aside from giving them a way to find meaning and purpose in captivity, to make some sense of it all, performing was fun for them too.

But there's always a spectre lingering somewhere within the account of any feast at Kobe House, waiting, ready to punish the hagiographer. And around the second week in May, Staff Sergeant Henry Ross, one of the hospital's RAMC medics made the unenviable transition from carer to patient. Of course, all the medics, including the doctors, were sick themselves, at one time or another, with diarrhoea, scabies, beriberi, and so on - the rolling gamut of disease and illness that was the POWs norm. But Ross's situation was especially dire, spiralling far beyond the medics' usual strategy of taking whatever medications might be available and then soldiering on.

Denton knew Ross very well, they had lived, slept, ate, and worked together, in the little hospital, twenty-four hours a day for a year and a half. Ross had overseen the hospital during the first four months after the *Lisbon Maru* survivors arrived at Kobe House, that first awful winter when the general state of health was at its worst, with men dying like flies, and the Japanese authorities at their most intransigent and belligerent. It was a rotten time for all the orderlies. But for Ross, faced with the responsibility of taking charge, it must have felt like carrying the weight of the world on his shoulders. And later, physically ill himself and still traumatised by the effects of the *Lisbon Maru* massacre, Ross suffered the effects of stress and had to be replaced as NCO in charge by Petty Officer Flynn.

For a soldier, and an RAMC medic is still very much a soldier, being relieved of command might have been resented and felt as a humiliation. The decision had been made by Major Houghton, the POW camp commandant. Houghton had been relieved that Ross took it all with good grace and still carried on doing his best in the hospital. Perhaps it was no surprise though, given that Ross had already palpably demonstrated the selflessness and courage needed to put the lives and welfare of the sick far above his own.

Looking back to when the POWs had finally escaped from the sinking *Lisbon Maru* most men, very understandably, had jumped off the ship. Some though, whether through being wounded by Japanese rifle fire, or being sick, diseased, and debilitated were unable to escape unaided. When Ross got out of the aft-hold he gathered some of these sick and injured men around him and did what he could to give first aid. Then Surgeon-Lieutenant Charles Jackson, a Royal Navy doctor, had climbed out from the forward hold, saw what Ross was doing and joined him.

Jackson and Ross stayed with the wounded until the ship finally went down, and then they tried to keep as many of the wounded men as they could afloat with them in the sea. They continued to look after the wounded men in the water for around four hours until they were finally picked up by the Japanese. Then, of course, Ross ended up at Kobe House setting up the hospital and teaching Denton and the other volunteers how to be orderlies. After the war Ross was awarded a posthumous Mention in Despatches (MiD). On Ross's memorial stone, his mother would choose the words 'he thought of others, never himself, gave his life helping his comrades,' which pretty much summed it up.

Ross, age twenty-six, now lay on a mat in his own hospital, suffering from a stomach ulcer, beriberi, malnutrition, and psychological trauma, no doubt enhanced by the litany of sores and skin diseases that had become too commonplace amongst POWs to excite much mention. It goes without saying that the medics did all they could for Ross, albeit to little effect. But the elephant in the room was that Ross was dying, and a man of his experience knows when his time has come. Of course, the doctors also knew, and the orderlies knew - everybody knew.

But there was nothing much else left that they could do or say. Indeed, what on earth could they say - not just to Ross, but to themselves. And, powerless to help, how does one sleep whilst listening to a friend, a few feet away, struggling for breath and gradually getting weaker and quieter as the night moves on.

To function at Kobe House hospital, men like Denton needed to acquire a veneer of external detachment. And in such situations, the emotional and psychological damage, an internal process building patient momentum for the future, even if felt or understood, is ignored, subsumed, and buried in the *now*. But Ross's death, one thinks, was different. Men became ill, men died, it was 'rotten luck,' but you'd done the best you could for them, and anyway, at least it wasn't you, it was someone else. Ross's departure though, would be a little too much challenge for the armour of detachment. This death had to be worse than the others - he was *inside* their band, and all men are not equal in death - it doesn't work like that.

Ross's ultimate cause of death was pulmonary infiltration, as recorded in his POW records. Hence Ross acted out the reality of his diagnosis, on 15th May, and finally choked to death as his lungs filled up with fluids, pus, or whatever else, and his organs failed. Denton, though, would have had little time to rage as his friend went off into the night. It was 4.40 p.m. on a Monday afternoon, the work parties were due back at camp, and the orderlies had twenty minutes or so to get themselves and the [other] patients ready for the small evening meal - and in food was life.

A TOUGH ACT TO FOLLOW

On the 1st of July 1944, Lieutenant Kazuo Takenaka took over as Camp Commandant from Morimoto. The POWs were paraded and given a speech in which Morimoto complimented them on their good spirits and promised that, subject to higher authority, he would do what he could to improve conditions for them. Though whether improvements came from Takenaka's new regime, Sergeant-Major Morita's supposedly liberal hand, or Major Houghton's quiet but persistent clawing in of administrative controls, or one of myriad other factors, was unlikely to overly concern Denton. More importantly, there would be improvements and concessions, and one of them was to allow the POWs to form a concert party that would be taken by lorry to Kobe POW Hospital, to entertain the patients there.

Kobe POW Hospital, newly formed, was something of a 'show hospital' and pet project of Colonel Sotaro Murata, the officer commanding all Osaka POW camps. The hospital was set up to replace the recently closed-down facility at Ichioka and, aside from a dire shortage of food, conditions at Kobe Hospital were markedly better than at its harsh predecessor. Whether this upgrade was prompted by a selfishly informed long-term eye looking ahead to post-war realities, or just propaganda to influence the International Red Cross is a matter of conjecture. Regardless, Heinrich Angst, the Red Cross representative was suitably impressed - or bamboozled perhaps - when he visited the hospital two days prior to the concert. His report, sent to

Zurich soon afterwards, praised the hospital and made much of Colonel Murata's deep concern for the health and welfare of the Osaka area POWs. Whether Denton saw things quite that way is rather less likely though, having witnessed so much needless death suffered on the colonel's watch. But for now, regardless of the byzantine politics, Denton focused on those things that were within his control, and he joined in the concert planning and preparation with gusto.

The concert at Kobe POW Hospital was held on a rest day, Sunday, the 20th August. The show kicked off with a medley performed by the Kobe House POW band. Captain Weedon - whose musical talents included taking mandolin lessons from Corporal Florence - was the officer who had been tasked with forming this band in an administrative sense. But musically, the band consisted of fifteen men under the leadership of Sergeant Jeffree, pragmatically equipped with an eclectic range of old instruments. The important thing here though is not whether the instruments were a bit of an odd collection, or whether they might have put out a few duff notes. What mattered for the musicians themselves, is that they had the chance to assert themselves as people not prisoners, to overcome their conditions, and then excel at something whilst in captivity.

The music, the songs, and the sketches, were all chosen with the intention of both uplifting the patients' spirits and amusing them with a bit of guarded satire, whilst at the same time not treading too hard on the volatile feelings of the Japanese Army. So, the band began its introductory medley with *Comrades*, an old favourite march, originating with the German Army. But the march's sentiment, it's allusion to friendship and going on to final victory were clear to men of the patients' background and generation.

The band followed on with some waltzes, but the sick and hungry men, especially being soldiers, were also looking for some light-hearted cheer – and they got this in full, and much appreciated, measure. It began with the *Busy Bee* sketch, based on Arthur Askey's popular 1938 performance of *The Bee Song*. This is about as silly as it can get, especially performed by soldiers and the antics of the busy little bee itself would have lent themselves nicely to some subtle anti-Japanese analogies. With the tone set, the *Busy Bee* was followed by some popular songs, and another comedy sketch, and then it was Denton's turn to perform as part of The Harmony Three.

The Harmony Three, their style, as the name suggests, sang together in harmony and unison. It was a unity that went far beyond the musical connotation though, as would be made plain forty years later when as comrades still they sang together in the smoky atmosphere of a Mansfield working mans' club. However, oblivious to the future and unconscious of the fanciful meanderings of biographers, the three men launched into an upbeat *Alexander's Ragtime Band* followed up with their version of *You'll Never Understand*.

The intensity of audience response, in its specifics, is lost to us now – though enjoyment, a moment of escape, that much is axiomatic for men starved of entertainment. For the patients, the music was a reminder that they were still alive, still men, that there was still a world with better things than cesspits, beatings, starvation and death. Whilst for Denton meaning came in the creative process, making music like making life, of itself no small import in a place where life was besieged, where caring and giving to others was some small measure of victory over inhumanity.

The trio finished up with the lively *There's Jazz in them there Horns*, then there were a couple of comedy sketches and some more band music. Not surprisingly, the patients, indeed all the POWs, loved comedy sketches. Denton and Florence joined in the sketches, though the main culprits were an iconoclastic group of nine men calling themselves The Mad Gang, who enjoyed risqué and risky Pythonesque tilting at their Japanese captors. Norman Colley, talented as both a performer and a song and sketch-writer, was arguably the artistic core of this group. And he and Denton were great friends, as were the other gang members who also appreciated Denton's infectious irrepressible sense of humour.

The concert progressed with more sketches from The Mad Gang, then a change of tone with a couple of ballads, *Stardust* and *That Distant Day*, from Florence. Picture the scene, Florence, a man who knew how to draw the poignant best out of any ballad, standing up on a small makeshift stage. The band, clutching their assorted instruments, sat in front, waiting. Then Denton, due on next, standing a little to the side with Colley, readying to go on. And the audience, the patients, orderlies, Doctor Page, [some of] the Japanese Army guards and administration, sat, stood, or lay on the ground, waiting for Florence to begin his second song.

Florence's song paints a picture of a man, and unstated, but assuredly, in the mind of the audience, the man is a soldier or sailor. He's promising a distant sweetheart that 'that distant day' will assuredly come and then they'll be together again. He sings how each night brings on 'an ache' which he deals with 'patiently,' in a sort of emotional one step process. This, of course, strikes right to the heart of the POWs' existential dilemma – the need to believe in the future and of better times to come, a belief that for many fuels the will to survive whilst, paradoxically, having to focus only on the now and the struggle to get through each day one at a time. Then he finishes up with...

> I look for that dawn and always say
> The hours that pass, so blue
> Only bring me closer to
> That distant – that certain, distant day.

It's not hard to envisage - as Florence slowly spun out the last notes of *certain, distant day* – more than a few moist eyes and a deafening moment of silence, followed by a round of applause that likely would have meant more to him than an Oscar ceremony.

No doubt Florence was a tough act to follow. But Denton, in show business one way or another from childhood onwards, was a pro. Norman Colley, who joined him sporting the wicked looking goat-like beard that the British Army would never had allowed him under normal circumstances was no slouch either. Their choice of songs was clearly thought through – the concert was intended to cheer the patients up, to boost the battered morale of men who were so ill that they stood out even within this environment where sickness was a norm.

So, to bring the mood back up and leave the patients on a high note, Denton and Colley finished with an upbeat extended version of *Sing a Song of Sixpence* – part of the outrageously cheerful lyrics of *Everybody Sing*, made popular in the 1930s by Hollywood star Judy Garland. Then, for a finale, the band rounded up with a medley of four tunes. The first one, *The Donkey Serenade*, continued the cheer-up tones of Denton and Colley, and when the trumpet sounded the 'he-haw' there would have been no doubt in any POWs' mind who the donkeys were! This was followed by some equally upbeat swing, with *South American Joe*. Then, to signify the concert was coming to an end, they played *Lights Out*, a poignant piece set to a poem written during the First World War.

To bring the concert to a close, the concert party would likely have preferred to have finished with the National Anthem. But unwilling to chance the rage of the guards in a different camp, they erred on the side of caution and chose *Land of Hope and Glory*, music whose accompanying words and political significance would be less likely to be understood and to provoke a negative response. Though, oddly enough, when back at Kobe House they generally could play the National Anthem at concerts and the [Japanese] guards there would happily join in with

God Save Our Gracious King.

The image of the sick emaciated prisoners at Kobe POW Hospital singing out the words of *Land and Hope and Glory*, with its description 'mother of the free,' may strike a mild note of irony [*to some*] now, given the POWs' actuality which was anything but free - a point that wouldn't have been lost on the men themselves. Nor, given the sweeping Japanese military victories, did anyone feel overly confident that God would make their country 'mightier yet' in the very near future. But the POWs, born long before the impositions of modern political correctness, were free to feel a little national pride, a brief jolt to their self-respect, whilst listening to the rousing tones played out by the POW band. And who can begrudge them, as for some men there the only real freedoms coming their way were those which death provides from hunger, pain, and fear.

A final irony to the day though is that Sergeant Major Morita may himself have performed in this concert: the enemy helping to bring comfort to the men suffering under the regime he was part of. In fact, he helped gain administrative permissions for the concerts to be held, frequently attended rehearsals, and participated in a few shows, fully aware that the sketches often reeked undertones of anti-Japanese humour.

LAST CHRISTMAS

Anyone familiar with war, imprisonment, or both, will know the importance of receiving mail, the feeling of connection, albeit brief, with home and family. POWs were, in theory at least, allowed to send and receive post via the International Red Cross. And Corporal Florence had received a letter from his sister back in March [1944] and replied to her in September, at one of the times that the Japanese administration decided to allow them to write a postcard home. Perhaps, as POWs often did, he shared his letter with his pal, Denton. But Denton himself received nothing from home, and often must have wondered why.

Of course, post between opposing combatant powers travelled by convoluted routes and was inevitably subject to such vagaries as downed aircraft and ships lost at sea. But another reason that some Kobe House POWs didn't receive mail was that the Japanese Army clerks at the headquarters in nearby Osaka, often looted the contents of parcels and burned large quantities of incoming and outgoing POW mail.

Whether Denton mourned his lack of postal connection, or conjectured imaginings about friends, family, home, bullet, bomb, and *blitzkrieg*, is itself nothing more than speculative probability. Undoubtedly though, the emotional import of the tiny handmade birthday card that he received on Tuesday 31st October from his friends in the Mad Gang stayed with him for the rest of his life. It was addressed to 'Muncy', an affectionate nickname bestowed by the Mad Gang because of his supposed resemblance to a 1930s American gangster of that name. All the gang signed the card, Colley, Helliadis, Welford, McDougall, and the rest.

The card itself was illustrated, and hand-written onto a piece of salvaged scrap paper, is full of doggerel verse validating friendship and urging hopes for the future. As a literary work the card might leave a little to be desired, but as a symbol of brotherhood and validation in a world where such things were hard earned, it was valued enough to be rescued and kept close in the chaos of the days ahead when Kobe House met its spectacular end, and then treasured through the years ahead until Joe met *his* end.

October was also conspicuous for an increase in the level of American air raids over Japan. In addition to having its own dock facilities, Kobe was close to Osaka, Japan's second largest port, so the city inevitably began to experience its share of the bombing. For the POWs, the sight of American bombers flying overhead brought on very mixed feelings. Conditions at Kobe House had indeed been improving, the level of gratuitous violence and punishment directed against the POWs had eased, and the death rate had fallen markedly. The POWs most certainly appreciated the improvements. But appreciation, in this context, is not the same as gratitude, and Denton, like every other POW, continued to wish death and destruction on the Japanese Empire – with the very specific exception of Kobe House. But kindly bombs exist only in the imaginings of poets. And when they fall, they kill impartially sparing neither bald young clerks nor prisoners of war. So, every unspoken prayer for revenge at Kobe House was tempered by the caveat known to anyone who has ever sat through any air-raid of any kind, in any war, 'please God, let it fall somewhere else.'

Apart from hopes for bloody retribution, the winter of 1944 also brought thoughts of Christmas - the POWs' third one at Kobe House. They were aware that the second front with the Allied invasion of occupied France had begun, and that Russian armies had Germany on the defensive in the east. And now American B29s were bombing the Japanese homeland. There's much, of course, that the POWs wished for, not least the destruction of Japan, the end of the war, and a return home. But the first Christmas had been a time without hope - little more than a hiatus in the winter of dying that followed in the aftermath of the *Lisbon Maru* massacre. The second Christmas, perhaps, had been a time more for reflection than celebration. Yet now, even the most guardedly pessimistic might see this Christmas at least as a Churchillian end of the beginning.

The rationale behind Colonel Morata's thinking re his end of year commemoration of his tenure as Officer Commanding the Osaka area POW camps was opaquer than that of the POWs. Fourteen Australian and British NCOs were ordered to remain in camp one day to write a funeral oration to honour the POWs who had died during the previous twelve months. The speech though, had to be written in the same tone and style as an analogous Japanese Army oration to the dead. So, the deaths of the POWs were eulogised and celebrated as glorious, righteous, and even enviable. The plan then being that once written the oration would take place on December 23rd at the Kobe POW hospital and be read out by Corporal Colley.

Denton's pal Colley was selected, no doubt, because of his speaking skills amply demonstrated at their concerts. But there was an irony in the oration which surely would have stuck in Denton's throat, having helped care for those sick and dying prisoners. To begin with, there is absolutely nothing glorious or patriotic in dying from disease and malnutrition. He knew full that most deaths at Kobe House had not only been eminently preventable, but that they resulted from the deliberate acts and omissions of the Japanese Army guards and administration. And, the final insult was that Colonel Morata, who ordered this travesty of a memorial, had had the power to have prevented the conditions that had caused these deaths.

Colley had had no choice about participating in Morata's commemoration, and so putting it behind him he joined Denton, Florence, and the rest of the little band of entertainers, in the weeks running up to Christmas, in planning a performance. They chose something traditional, a pantomime concert, *very* loosely based on the story of Aladdin, but toned to appeal to the soldierly mind. Then they wrote a show frenzied with double entendres and named it *Charlie's Ring*, inserting as much topical anti-Japanese satire as they thought might fly under the administrative radar.

Putting together a show on the scale that they eventually achieved took the efforts of a great many men who worked, connived, and took real personal risks to make it all happen, though the POWs themselves were also quick to acknowledge that Norman Colley and Joe Denton were leading lights in the process. As a child actor, one of Denton's roles had been in a comedy revue at the Alhambra Theatre in 1932. The revue included scenes such as the Arabian Dance, which experience now stood him in good stead, choreographing the rather more risqué offerings like the dance of the seven veils in *Charlie's Ring*,

Locating the items needed for a pantomime production in a country by now economically ravaged and denuded of goods by wartime blockades and bombing, and then separating them from their civilian owners whilst out on working parties was mission enough. And, theatrical props aside, it's a saddening thought that by this stage of the war much of the Japanese civilian populace were existing on just as poor (and sometimes even poorer) rations as the Kobe House POWs. Though, dire as the POWs' conditions were, thanks to Houghton's [and others'] efforts to run the camp as it should be, Kobe House was one of Osaka's better organised and provided for POW camps. In fact, by comparison to other camps, morale at Kobe House was quite high, so much so that the Kempeitai [a sort of Japanese Gestapo], suspicious that there was some other factor at play, sent in a spy masquerading in the role of interpreter.

By now Kobe House's POW body collective was as accomplished a collection of thieves and smugglers as might have been found anywhere outside of one of His Majesty's Prisons back in England. Their task, which they accomplished at far greater personal risk than this little detour into levity might suggest, was to 'acquire' a collection of ladies clothing, silk fabrics, gold jewellery, and sundry other bits and pieces. They then had to smuggle these items past the guards and into the camp, where they were hidden away inside one of the attics where the cast could work at turning them into costumes and props.

The weeks before Christmas were spent, when opportunity presented, in planning, rehearsing, and generally preparing the show. To add to this, they had to improvise a stage and curtains, and even a dressing room, using bedding, whilst Colley [a Royal Engineer] who remained in camp each Monday to do repairs and maintenance, rigged up an improvised spotlight. For some of the men, putting together a three-hour pantomime and show under any circumstances, not to mention within a POW camp, was an experience they had never envisaged doing in their wildest dreams. For Denton, who had been performing on stage since his childhood as a professional entertainer in theatres and music halls, and more recently in garrison concerts and even Hong Kong radio, it was his bread and butter. And for all of them, it was a chance for a little while at least, to live in a different story where the genie gets firmly stuffed back into the bottle and the forty thieves are lovable rogues, innocent of nothing except beriberi!

Christmas Day, this year, arrived on a Monday, which was normally a workday, though the Japanese administration had allowed a holiday, which was made up for by working the previous rest day [Sunday]. There were some men at Kobe House who sincerely and deeply celebrated the day as the birth of Jesus Christ. Others though, if they had ever been truly religious, had lost their faith in unanswered appeals for help in the black airless cargo holds onboard the *Lisbon Maru*, or whilst crunching barefoot across a maggot strewn floor to void bloodied faeces in Kobe House's overflowing pit latrine.

Florence, a Catholic, held on to more spirituality than Denton, who was more the secularist and less enthused for attending church services. The services were generally conducted by Captain Dibb, a career officer, and former Royal Tank Corps trooper who'd come up from the ranks, had served in the Army for twenty-three years, and was older than many of the other soldiers. Dibb, a deeply religious man, had been brought up in Merthyr Tydfil and likely influenced by its sense of non-conformity and lay traditions. Regardless, he functioned as a sort of lay preacher for all Christian faiths at Kobe House, which contrasted a little oddly perhaps with his role as a soldier, albeit now a Royal Engineer. On some occasions the Japanese administration also provided an ordained Japanese Christian priest for services and ceremonies, though the men's preference likely leaned more towards the spiritually junior but nationally correct ecumenicalism offered by Dibb.

Christmas for most everyone, spiritual or not, brought thoughts of home and family, recollection and nostalgia, and for some perhaps far more sadness than anything else. It was also three years to the day that Denton had gone into captivity following the surrender of Hong Kong, which was hardly a cause for festive joy. Mail had been issued early that morning, mostly letters from wives and parents for those men whose post had survived the attentions of the censors or the letter-burning of the Japanese Army clerks at HQ. Regardless, we can be sure though that Denton received nothing from his parents. His mother had died eight years earlier, and although Denton wasn't aware of this yet, his father, a reserved Victorian character likely much damaged by his own experiences in the trenches during the First World War, had died in 1941.

As a child, Denton's father's outward expression of father-son bonding had generally been limited to having his son trotted out on Sundays for a stilted paternal interchange. And neither father nor son had been too visibly distraught during a restrained goodbye when Denton joined the Army, three days after his eighteenth birthday. But that doesn't mean that neither one cared at all, nor would it stop the feelings of aloneness hidden away behind brash soldierly insouciance at the sound of another 'sorry mate, nothing for you,' Christmas mail call.

But within the little hospital, Denton and the other medics and orderlies, sucked up personal sorrows and did what they could to inject a bit of festive cheer with some decorations and a small Christmas tree that the Japanese commandant allowed them to buy. The duty medic(s) had been awake during the night of Christmas Eve, the remainder started their day at 6.30 a.m. followed by the 7.00 a.m. Tenko, and then the time was their own. That said, patients still needed to be cleaned, and fed, and given nursing and medical treatment, and the psychiatric patients still required constant supervision. Though the psychological damage was not confined to those men diagnosed clinically insane by Doctor Boyce. A while back, one unfortunate patient, whose mental and physical agonies were far from unique, had tried to commit suicide by throwing himself down a lift shaft, unable to cope any more with the pain caused by beriberi.

Now though, Denton and Florence no doubt had bits and pieces to do getting ready for the afternoon concert, and one way or another, the hospital was busy enough. But that day at least, they had some food, some leisure, and enough insight into the progress of the war to think that if starvation, disease, or captor's caprice didn't kill them during the following year, that this might be their last Christmas as POWs.

Eating that day, not just in the hospital of course, but for all the POWs, was special as they broke out a few hoarded and hidden smuggled items to add to whatever had been saved back from the Red Cross Parcels that had been given out earlier that month. It's hard, maybe impossible, for those of us who have at worst only ever briefly experienced hunger, to comprehend the joy that some simple foods bring to men who have balanced on the edge of real starvation for three years. For Denton and Florence, these small treats, a piece of chocolate, perhaps a coffee or tea first thing before breakfast, or some tinned cheese to go with the two small bread rolls issued at lunch, made this a truly red-letter day.

Most men rested after lunch, relaxing, talking, reminiscing, and looking forward to the concert. Then, straight after the 4.30 p.m. (early) tea of horsemeat soup, they all gathered on the third floor, six hundred or so prisoners, miseries forgotten for a while, with a buzz of anticipation as the performers readied behind the curtains.

The little orchestra, much practiced over the previous weeks, warmed up in time honoured fashion, then the show began. The curtain, or blankets to be strictly accurate, went up on a scene showing two prisoners at Kobe House, played by two of the Mad Gang, Petty Officer Henry Short, as 'Shortie,' and Stoker Petty Officer Reginald Thorne, as 'Charlie.' The two characters were sat having a chat before bed. Charlie, who worked at Sempaku, a company involved in loading and unloading ships in Kobe docks, where many of the POWs had actually worked at one time or another, had 'found' a ring whilst on a work party, and he was polishing it up whilst showing it to his friend.

The result of the soldierly cleaning and polishing was predictable, albeit not quite as Antoine Galland might have envisaged. The genie appears and explains the ring's standard operating procedure of rub, wish, and receive, and then fulfils the obligatory demand for food, bottles of beer, and cigarettes! It's safe to assume that there was then no shortage of suggestions from the audience regarding what else to wish for, some of which are probably better left to the imagination. However, the two men decided to ask for a trip to a New York nightclub, where they meet the 'stars.' Then the Mad Gang, and Denton (as part of the Harmony Three), did various skits on the night club theme, including a 'famous' violinist, a celebrity dance couple, and a band led by Florence.

For reasons that nobody inquired too deeply into, Charlie and Shortie then asked the genie to take them back to their trouble filled childhood at school. The school was run by an incompetent and immoral headmaster and teachers, based on comedic characters instantly recognisable to the POWs from cinema and radio. And from there it wouldn't have taken much imagination to realise that the skit was satirising the dishonesty and incompetence of many of the Japanese guards and the industry honchos [foremen]. As for the POWs, the fun was all the better for seeing some of these same guards sat laughing away in the audience not realising that the joke was on them. Perhaps the jewel in this satirical crown though, was a little piece of slapstick so obvious that it successfully flew in plain sight under the Japanese administrative radar.

Lance Corporal Albert 'Rosie' Jefford, a Royal Engineer, played the role of a schoolboy arriving late for class. Jefford, inevitably looking ridiculous in homemade schoolboy shorts and a cap, came into class and faced the hysterical temper of the headmaster, a tilt at the behaviour of some of the guards and work foremen when they were angered. But the schoolboy, clearly prepared, revealed a daikon – a detested 'stew to death' vegetable that the POWs were often fed on in lieu of anything more nutritious. To the knowing cheers and laughter of the audience, the schoolboy presented the daikon, something they had grown to loath, as a gift to the quickly mollified headmaster, all of which the POWs recognised as mocking Japanese corruption and bribe-taking.

The school scene was followed by a string of ever more ridiculous scenarios as Charlie and Shortie ended up in Baghdad, vicariously fulfilling the imaginings of the watching soldiers. With hundreds of men crammed into a restricted space it was baking hot, and one envisages a plethora of unanticipated problems with sweating performers and Heath Robinson make-up running on the faces of painted 'ladies' in the Sultan's harem. The audience were in no mood to pick holes though; nor even were the Japanese guards and camp administration sat in the front row, realising that almost every item of clothing and scenery that they saw must have been stolen outside and then smuggled past them into camp.

By this stage, Colley and Denton, who'd taken a leading role in putting it all together had every reason to feel pleased with themselves, as did everyone else involved on both sides of the curtain. And, so, the finale ran on with Charlie and Shortie's snake dance, various shenanigans with eastern ladies, and a most unamused Sultan watching from his cushioned dais. Private Helliadis followed on singing *All of Me*, a song with lyrics rich in innuendo when delivered by a tough infantryman hammed up in drag. Then he brought the house down doing the dance of the seven veils, just before Shorty and Charlie's wives appear. Sooner than face their wives, the boys summoned the genie and demanded to be taken back to Kobe House, where they give the ring back to the genie and go to bed. Then in the morning they wake up to the sounds of reveille and discover that the genie has left them a Red Cross parcel in return for giving back the ring.

No doubt the end of the panto was marked by curtain calls and all the usual goings on at such occasions, then the senior officers came up and did their bit. Lieutenant Takenaka, the Camp Commandant, wished the POWs well and hoped that they would soon be reunited with their families. Then Major Houghton read out various messages delivered him via the International Red Cross. The messages, predictable in content, and non-contentious by necessity, were appreciated by the POWs, nonetheless. General George C. Marshall, the American Chief of Staff, thanked all the American POWs 'for their steadfast courage and faith.' Mackenzie King, the Canadian Prime Minister, told how the Canadian people 'eagerly awaited the POWs return.' The Australian government, expressed how 'the people of Australia ... looked forward to the day when you will be reunited with us.'

Major Houghton even had a message from the Indian Red Cross to read out, which no doubt surprised the two Indians in the audience, part of a small group of odd nationalities captured at sea aboard British merchant ships. The Indian Red Cross, eschewing orthodoxy in favour of seasonality, wished their two compatriots 'Christmas greetings and best wishes for early reunion and a happy New Year.' Though after watching, Denton, Florence, Colley, and the rest cavorting around in what must have seemed the oddest spectacle to anyone unversed in the art of pantomime, the two Indian seamen were likely beyond being surprised by anything!

Having done his duty to the American, Australian, and Canadian POWs, Houghton was left with a problem. There were a handful of Merchant Marine sailors, Greeks, an Argentinian, a Maltese, and an Egyptian in the audience, who probably hadn't expected anything from their respective governments - not to mention four Chinese men also captured at sea. Though the Chinese were likely content to have avoided the same fate as millions of their countrymen, killed under Japanese military occupation during the previous few years. But Houghton was also faced with around 375 British POWs wondering why they were left unmentioned amongst the Christmas greetings. Houghton was in no position to know whether messages had been sent out by the British government. So, to the British POWs' satisfaction, he said that the British Prime Minister, Winston Churchill, was busy with other matters far more important than themselves – by inference, winning the war – and so brought the evening to a happy close.

1945

February 1945 arrived accompanied by heavy snow, an unwelcome seasonal visitor. Far worse, and, unknown to the POWs, on February 4th in some distant planning room the Valkyries elected Kobe for a carpet-bombing trial of incendiary bombs. The firebombing plans were equally unknown to Captain Donald Longbottom RAMC, a British Army doctor transferred to Kobe House from Amagasaki twelve days later. Longbottom may not have been pleased about being sent to Kobe House, had he known. But given that some of his peers at Amagasaki were later sent to Hiroshima, it might not have been such a bad thing.

When Boyce had arrived at Kobe House, it had been a relief to the orderlies to have a doctor to take charge of the POWs' medical care. Longbottom was now less of a boon in that sense, but he did bring something with him that in some ways was almost as important as medical expertise –news of the outside world and of the conditions that other POWs experienced. Longbottom had been captured in Singapore and had been sent to work on the infamous Death Railway, built to link Thailand with Burma, and then sent out to Japan. Longbottom hadn't been trained as a surgeon though, he was a general practitioner. But his time on the Railway had taught him some tough lessons in surgical techniques which quickly became known amongst the troops. For instance, boils and abscesses were endemic due to malnutrition, and he cheerfully lanced or cut these out without anaesthetic. So before sick parade, many of the sufferers would ask the orderlies who the duty doctor was and then not report sick if it was Longbottom.

Denton had been forced to do some amateur surgery himself on at least one occasion. POWs often suffered from sores and ulcers that rotted down to the bone or went gangrenous. And, in the lack of adequate medical facilities, these sores sometimes worsened to the extent of causing limb amputation. Once Denton had had use a penknife to cut off a man's rotted toe which, to his surprise, as he recalled later, came off so easily.

Aside from a penchant for tough love surgery, Longbottom earned a reputation for being pleasant and affable and someone that the orderlies could talk to and learn from. Longbottom and Denton also shared a love of sport. Denton was a keen amateur boxer, athlete, and footballer. Longbottom, however, was a well-known league cricketer, so there was plenty of scope for some friendly banter between the two men. Longbottom was also a chess player with a keen intellect, though he likely enjoyed less cerebral forms of entertainment too. And no doubt he'd have been in the audience along with everyone else when the usual crowd, including Denton, put on a concert - a farce - early in the evening of March 11th after tea.

Unknown to Kobe House's thespians though, two days earlier on the 9th March, Major General Curtis LeMay, commanding the US XXI Bomber Command, had decided to switch tactics from conventional high-altitude strategic bombing and instead began a series of maximum effort low-level night incendiary attacks on major Japanese industrial cities – one of them being Kobe. And pretty much as soon as the concert finished, the air-raid alarm sounded followed by a series of small raids leading to a much-disturbed night.

Tokyo and Nagoya were the first full-scale beneficiaries of LeMay's new tactics, with Tokyo, as the pilots described it, catching fire like a forest of pine trees. Then, on 13th March, Osaka was visited by 275 B29s flying over in waves throughout the night and leaving behind them over eight square miles of total devastation. This was only around fifteen miles away, as the bomber flies, from Kobe House. Accordingly, the POWs were ordered to get dressed and pack their scanty kit and belongings ready to evacuate the building in the eventuality that a raid came their way. Once readied, the men lay on their sleeping platforms bundles to hand and awaited events. Some men listened to the sounds of Osaka being hammered, trying to gauge progress. Others, skilled in the soldierly art of grabbing what sleep you can when you can, did their best to sleep through it until the sounds finally petered out in the early hours of the following morning. But the impact of the noise, the smoke, the smells, from destruction on this scale were inescapable. And it wasn't too hard to guess that Kobe, Japan's fourth most important industrial base and the deep-water port for central Japan, would be due for its share soon enough too.

But whilst the napalm was raining down on Osaka, Kobe House, or at least its commandant, blissfully accepted a more welcome gift, a venerable, worn-out, and tiny little Austin Seven car. Occasions of shared good humour between captors and captives were few and far between but, this was one of those times. Seemingly Lieutenant Takenaka rolled up in a venerable and dilapidated Austin – a wonderful old British manufactured car, but one whose diminutive size had made it the butt of music hall comedians and seaside post-cards. And the image follows on of a little man, clutching a big sword, tripping out of a tiny rickety car, surrounded by grinning Japanese and Allied soldiers trying not laugh too openly.

There was some talk that Takenaka would use one of the POWs as a chauffeur. Car ownership before the war was limited by comparison to today, and many of the soldiers couldn't drive. But Denton, most unusually for an enlisted man, had owned a sports car in Hong Kong prior to the invasion and could drive. He wasn't tempted to volunteer as a driver though, but he did help his much talented pal, Colley, to compose a song in the car's honour.

Denton and Colley sang their song at one of the rest day concerts. The song lampooned the car, mentioning its gifted provenance and its being used by Takenaka to carry around his 'geisha girl' girlfriend. The song followed on with a verse that the POWs enjoyed, but that likely raised Japanese hackles:

> The engine is so very good – the best you've ever seen.
> It doesn't run on charcoal [as many wartime Japanese vehicles had to] – no, it uses gasoline.
> And when they want to oil it, they use Red Cross shaving cream.

The implication of this was that the Japanese guards in general, and the camp commandant, Takenaka, were looting the POWs' Red Cross parcels. This was undoubtedly true - but mentioning it made Takenaka lose face. Another verse included the lines,

> The chauffeur's got a big red ring,
> The driving seat[s] got just one spring.

The song is truly funny - it was topical and satirical, and included enough smut to appeal to the soldierly mind. Clearly Takenaka didn't see it that way though, the concert was immediately stopped, and Denton and Colley were marched off to the guardroom. The two men were made to stand to attention until the following day. They'd brought the house down, albeit not quite the way they had planned. But their punishment could have been much worse, and it's likely that this was one of those times where the intercession of the theatre loving Sergeant Major Morita was successful.

On the 16th of March three-hundred-and-six American B29 Superfortress bombers came to Kobe, each of them flying individual sorties at somewhere between five thousand to eight thousand feet. Their undersides had been painted black to obscure shine and so lesson target visibility to the Japanese anti-aircraft batteries. Most of the POWs felt that these Americans knew that they were there and that they were avoiding dropping bombs in the vicinity of Kobe House. And they were right in part - the location of the camp was known to the Allies. Though, even assuming the Americans had been trying to avoid the camp, the POWs would have been far less sanguine if they had understood more about the realities of accurate aerial bombing. Regardless, as one does at such times, the POWs vacillated between wanting to get under shelter or wanting to see and know what was going on.

The sirens had gone off around 11.30 p.m. Denton was sleeping in the little hospital along with the patients, and the other medics, plus Captain Boyce. Sergeant Major Morita came around and ordered all the POWs to get dressed and to pack their kit. Then the medics got the patients ready, keeping a close eye on the psychiatric cases, and prepared what medical stores they had in readiness for dealing with bomb and burn injuries.

Initially, the POWs were taken out to the little park on the opposite side of the small road in front of Kobe House where the air raid shelter trenches had been dug. Some Japanese civilians joined them until, sometime later, the POWs were ordered back inside the building. If the POWs had then been allowed to continue watching from the dubious vantage point of the buildings' third floor windows, and if they could have actually seen through the roiling clouds of smoke and flame, they would have been able to witness around 2,328 tons of enhanced-formula Napalm B, helped on by some added air-burst fragmentation bombs, turning the two-and-a-half square miles of cityscape stretching between them and the docks into little more than cinders and ashes. However, Sergeant [later Sergeant Major] Tatsuhiko Furuya had other ideas and issued orders that the POWs were not to look out of the windows.

Furuya, was known to the POWs as the Pay Sergeant, quite simply because that was his official post within the Japanese Army camp administration. Not exactly renowned for his patience at the best of times, and someone who seemed to wield authority within the camp well above his rank, Furuya was running on a particularly short fuse that day. And one of the practical manifestations of this is that he'd replaced the wooden Kendo practice sword, that he generally used for beating men, with a long metal bar instead. Whether the replacement was made of iron or steel was a moot point for Denton though. He would soon witness the bar's effects on Private Abrahams, one of the other POWs, little knowing that it foreshadowed his own steel-crossed fate.

Recollections differ, after the war some men recalled the Abraham's beating as happening during an earlier raid whilst others fix it clearly on this day. Suffice then that it happened during a raid, when the POWs were inside the building, the lights were switched off, iron shutters were placed over the windows, and the doors were locked and bolted from the outside. For Denton and pals this was unpleasantly reminiscent of being trapped inside the sinking *Lisbon Maru*. Not surprisingly then, some of the men were nervous about the situation and wanted to be near an exit, whilst others wanted to know what was happening outside.

By now there was no electricity as the supply had failed due to the bombing. It shouldn't have mattered given that it was daytime now and so there were no longer black-out implications. But the Japanese administration still forbad looking through or opening any of the windows. So, the POWs continued sitting inside the dimly lit buildings waiting for events to unfold. In Block A, an Australian soldier, Private Abrahams, took a chance and looked through a gap in one of the steel window-shutters trying to catch a glimpse of bombers whose sound could be heard passing overhead. No doubt Abrahams wasn't the only man to sneak a glance out the windows, but he was the one unfortunate enough to be seen doing it by the Pay Sergeant as he sneaked around looking for miscreants to vent his fears and frustrations on.

Screaming in anger Furuya ordered Abrahams to go outside to the guardroom, an action that often resulted in some form of violence, and this time was no exception. Furuya began by thrashing Abrahams with a metal rod until he collapsed unconscious, then brought him round with buckets of cold water and continued the beating until he ran out of bile and allowed Abrahams to be carried away to the hospital. So, when Furuya made it clear that he would kill the next man he saw trying to look out of a window, the threat would have felt very real to the medical orderlies and the other POWs.

Normality gradually resumed over the next few days as the electricity was restored, outside work details were resumed, and the POWs, whose official rations had been reduced even further, were even issued with a Red Cross parcel. Normality though was an odd concept for the POWs, especially in the little hospital where Denton took his turn caring for the psychiatric cases – men literally driven insane by the totality of their experiences on the *Lisbon Maru* and in captivity. And so, life continued at Kobe House and they all slid further down the rabbit hole with Denton and pals working in the hospital, dazed civilians wandering around their half-obliterated city, whilst downed American airmen faced a black-capped kangaroo court up on the hill overlooking Kobe.

All through the previous night fellow Allied POWs and internees had watched the bombing from their own camp higher up on the hills that framed Kobe House to the north. Impressed, they later described Kobe's introductory Gotterdammerung as being like night turned into day with the flames literally bright enough to read a newspaper by. Their enthusiasms were tempered somewhat though when one B29 disintegrated above them after being rammed by a Japanese fighter plane, and bodies floated down preceded by the burning wreckage. The dead airmen were collected up and lay on the ground for four days under Japanese guard. However, two of the crew, Staff Sergeant Algy Auganas and Lieutenant Robert Nelson, survived, albeit with some injuries, and they parachuted down, were taken prisoner and a few days later were tried, sentenced, and executed.

Thereon the Kobe bombing raid was completed, with napalm melted civilians, dead Americans falling from the sky, and the POWs in Kobe House surrounded by a city in ruins and now tasked with preparing a concert to honour the Son of Heaven's forthcoming birthday. No one had planned the war quite this way, certainly not the unfortunate POWs, nor even the Emperor himself. Nonetheless, events ground inexorably on towards the final act and so Denton et al. prepared the musical accompaniment.

The 29th April 1945 was the Japanese Emperor's Birthday. It's quite difficult now with the remove of time and generation to appreciate the degree of reverence, bordering on worship, that the Japanese emperor was held in by his nation. It was clear enough, from whispered conversations and changing behaviours, that civilians in Kobe were war weary. Nonetheless, even at this stage of the war, with the country on the edge of ruin, the Emperor's birthday was an extremely special occasion. And, as such, it would be celebrated accordingly.

The men at Kobe House who put on the concerts, Colley, Florence, Denton, and many others, knew all too well that their captors were living on a knife edge and that temperaments, mercurial at best, were better left unprovoked, especially on the big dog's special day. But change could be felt in the wind. Only a few days earlier one of the camp guards had been seen stealing a Red Cross parcel from the stores due to be distributed to the POWs. It's possible that he was one of the government-employed civilian guards, and hence of lower status within the Japanese camp hierarchy than the army guards, which might then have influenced the following events. Nonetheless, he'd been grabbed by a POW and taken in front of Major Houghton, the *British* camp administrator and seemingly the Japanese guard had literally gone down on his knees and begged not to be reported to his [Japanese] superiors – something that would have been unimaginable even a few months earlier. Of course, all sorts of interpretations might be attached to this. Whilst it was true that many Japanese people were losing confidence in the eventual outcome of the war, it might also be that it was a reflection of the strength and effectiveness of the administration slowly and painstakingly built up by Houghton and his team, or perhaps on this occasion the Japanese commandant had even banned the guards from their usual pilfering of the Red Cross stores.

The entertainers had sailed close to the wind before, though not always totally successfully. For instance, in a concert held the previous June, they had included a short sketch of a working party labouring on the docks. During the skit a comedic Japanese guard punished one of the men for some transgression or other. The POW audience found it hilarious, though the Japanese camp staff also watching were far less amused and the actors were stood rigidly to attention in front of the guardhouse for two hours after the show. By Japanese Army standards, this was a very mild punishment. But that said, Furuya, the Pay Sergeant, hadn't been at Kobe House then.

The day started earlier than usual, at around 4.30 am, when more than six hundred POWs were paraded on the road outside the camp waiting to bow towards the east – the direction of both the Emperor's palace in Tokyo and the rising sun. After this the prisoners were taken on a somewhat less reverential walk scavenging for salvageable items amongst the dead horses and general detritus littering the bombed-out buildings around

Kobe House. And it wasn't too hard to see that the sun would be setting soon enough, and that the time of obeisance might soon be over - a thought that may have spurred Joe Denton to push his luck a little too far during the concert later that evening.

The concert started well enough as Mister Goat brought the house down with some stand-up comedy. There was a skit parodying two Japanese bureaucrats in competition to see who could wear the most official armbands, that went down well with the POWs at least. Morita, the camp sergeant major, liked sketches like this and laughed along with the rest. But it was the next sketch satirising a Japanese work foreman stealing bags of sugar that was the tipping point. Furuya, the Pay Sergeant, was perched amongst the Japanese soldiers in the front row of the audience. He exploded with rage, screaming and shouting, and ordered all the performers to stand in front of the stage. Then with hundreds of prisoners sat behind him, frustrated and helpless, unable to intervene, Furuya ranged up and down the line, visiting violence on Colley, Florence, the Mad Gang, Denton, and the rest of the cast.

Lashing about him with fists and boots, Furuya went on and on inflicting pain and injury until he quite literally had no more strength left to keep going. Then the men were marched away and paraded in front of the guardhouse. Furuya then took a metal rod and lashed at the men with it whilst they stood to attention, as best they could. It likely seems almost incomprehensible to think that men could remain standing still without defending themselves whilst a raging lunatic kicks them or beats them with an iron bar. But Denton just had to dig deep into the finite reservoir of courage that sustains a man at such times, and so he stood there silently with the rest, knowing that any resistance would likely lead to his death.

Furuya was about five foot six inches tall, a similar height to Denton. His rage still not spent, he faced Denton and swung the iron bar towards him. Instinctively this time, Denton lifted his arm up palm outwards and took the force of the blow inside his left forearm. It was a strong enough blow to tear the flesh open for six inches and would have numbed the arm, rendering it useless for a while.

One might very reasonably ask why by now, or long before really, someone hadn't reined Furuya in. Major Houghton, who *might* have been able to do something, had been transferred away to Ikuno a month earlier along with the rest of the [Allied] officers. Morita, who was the [Japanese] camp sergeant major would have liked to have intervened. But Furuya was senior to him in rank or seniority, and so Morita was powerless to bring things under control. And the man who really should have put a stop to what by now was turning into a war crime, Lieutenant Takanaka, the camp commandant, abrogated responsibility leaving Furuya unchecked.

One might wonder too what thoughts ran through the minds of this close-knit group of friends standing there whilst Furuya raged up and down the line: gut-wrenching fear perhaps as he approaches, and the rotten guilty feeling of relief when he shifts attention from you and focuses the toe of his boots on your mate standing alongside. And one might ponder on the mental processes going on in Furuya's mind as he tortured defenceless men, righteously convinced that *he*, Furuya, was the injured party. One might also weep that mankind can engender cultures which breed creatures like this and then allows them full rein.

Such meanderings mattered not one iota at the time, the reality was that in this criminally negligent vacuum of command and control, Furuya, infuriated by Denton's defiance, could swing the bar again and again. And this time it smashed down on Denton's forehead slicing through the skin and fracturing the frontal [skull] bone above his left eye. Thereon the punishment of the other men carried on whilst Denton, unconscious, lay on the ground, liberated by blunt force trauma. Eventually, though, Denton was carried off to hospital and the other men were crammed into a cell for the rest of the night.

It's odd perhaps, at this stage, to think of Denton as being fortunate, beaten unconscious and lying with a fractured skull in the makeshift hospital. The potential complications of a cranial fracture from swelling, bleeding, or infection are dire. But Denton had none of these problems, and he regained consciousness in the room where he had tended so many others himself over the last couple of years. And the following morning, whilst Denton continued to recover in the hospital, the men in cells were released and sent to work though warned they would be locked up again at the end of the day. Then, to cap it all, the sun rose on an unseasonably warm day and sat like a bright red symbolic cliché in the sky, whilst later a single B29 bomber flew across the city and dropped its bombs. So ended the last concert at Kobe House.

Part of the fallout from the concert was that a couple of days later the concert party had to write a letter of apology to the camp commandant. Aside from signing it, Denton had little to do with drafting the letter. In fact, Sergeant Major Morita came forward and helped the men to write it. Morita told Colley that it would be better that way as he knew what the commandant wanted to hear. Morita also told Colley that he was sorry that the concert party had been beaten up. He went on to say that the Pay Sergeant didn't understand the POWs in the way that he [Morita] did, but that because Furuya was senior to him there had been nothing he could have done to stop the beatings. But now that tempers had calmed, Morita did at least manage to use his influence to stop the men from having to spend any more time in jail.

Morita was no saint himself, he physically punished men when caught stealing or contravening camp regulations. But by Japanese Army mores his punishments were lawful, minor, and they were always controlled and commensurate. In fact, Morita turned a blind eye to a good deal of rule infringement by the entertainers. Morita liked music and entertainment and sometimes played a role in concerts himself. But his treatment of the entertainers wasn't simple favouritism, as a camp sergeant-major he generally treated all the men fairly and the POWs were always pleased when Morita was doing the inspections, or if it was Morita on duty during an air raid and so on. But Morita got to know the concert performers probably better than he did the rest of the POWs. And he couldn't have known it - but the small kindnesses and humanity shown them, in a place where such virtues were in very short supply, would be repaid one day by some of Denton's fellow performers, men like Colley, Owen, Helladic, Welford, and Short.

More immediately, for the POWs, the coming month of May [1945] might have felt perhaps, like the continuation of a world governed by the Maniae. The sturdy brick-built Kobe House stood itself untouched within a shattered landscape devoid of the many buildings that *had* been made of wood prior to the fire-bombing. Birds began to sing nonetheless, and trees budded and blossomed along the edge of streets swept clear of the rubble from sometime still smoking ruins. Work parties continued to be sent through these same streets, out to what was left of the increasingly dysfunctional docks and factories, marching past the German Consulate where the swastika flag flying at half-mast, in mourning for Adolf Hitler's death, trumpeted the fate of Germany writ clear. And their Japanese Army captors, busily fiddling still, issued yet more regulations including an order that any prisoner found chewing gum as they marched through the ruined city would be severely punished.

Through the following weeks some men were transferred out whilst other men were transferred in - amongst them many extremely sick and debilitated American servicemen, some of whom were put into the hospital. One of these American soldiers also needed to have a toe amputated, and as a result developed tetanus and was unable to open his mouth to eat. Lacking antibiotics, muscle relaxants, intra-venous giving sets, and all the other paraphernalia that one would normally expect as a given, this left the orderlies with a dilemma, how to get food and fluids into the patient – something that can't be delayed in nutritionally challenged prison camp inmates. So, Denton broke his teeth – a painful, but lifesaving action and the man survived and later thanked Denton for what he'd done.

By June it was clear to Denton and everyone else that the war was grinding inexorably to a close. News bulletins were filtering in from Japanese civilians and workers, and the sound of nearby Osaka being hammered by B29 bombers spoke its own reality. And the inmates of Kobe House who, aside from the bulk of British, American, and Australians, included [a few] men from myriad nations and religions, all united in praying to a pantheon of Gods for a speedy Allied victory and a crushing Japanese defeat.

But with the prospect of an Allied victory came underlying fears for the POWs own safety. Aside from the concern of being immolated in the next big raid, whose coming was blindingly obvious, the men feared what their captors might do to *them* in the final hours of a Japanese defeat. It was a rational concern, a very real possibility that they would be executed if Japan was invaded. So, it was a good thing perhaps that the POWs were unaware that the Japanese high command had already issued orders to this very effect, and that elsewhere some POWs had been massacred by the Japanese Army to prevent them being liberated. And whilst out on work parties, some men had already been given informal warnings. Though at Kobe House Denton heard the words, 'Americanos come – you die' so often that, paradoxically, they seemed to lose meaning. But deep inside, Denton, and anyone else who had the words *Lisbon Maru* burned into their soul, well understood the reality of such threats.

The date chosen by the United States Army Air Force XXI Bomber Command to re-visit Kobe's industrial area was 5th June 1945. It was an auspicious day for the bomber crews – exactly one year since the first use of B29s in combat when they had bombed railway facilities in Thailand. Oblivious to all this, the POWs sat down to breakfast, scraping the few miserable grains of rice from their bowls in the usual manner. Around 5.45 a.m. they heard the general air raid alarm, signifying a raid in the Kobe area, prompting mixed emotions of worries for their own survival whilst at the same time wishing death and destruction on the military machine keeping them there.

Furuya, the Pay Sergeant, an especial focus for some of these less than fraternal wishes, ordered the men to go to their quarters and pack their kit ready to move out. It took very little time for most men to roll up a few items of clothing and the odd personal item, and that done they lay waiting, thinking, with perhaps some men throwing up the odd prayer. The hospital staff, doctors and orderlies, had a well-rehearsed drill which they put into practice, packing up their little stock of instruments and medicines and preparing the patients for possible evacuation. Then around half an hour later the nearby anti-aircraft guns opened-up, and the local air-alarm sounded a wailing statement of the obvious to warn of an immediate local raid.

The sound, the concussion, the ear-splitting noise of artillery at close quarters needs to be experienced to be appreciated. Denton likely listened and understood with the artilleryman's professional ear. Though the thoughts of the unfortunate patients are more difficult to probe, especially the psychiatric cases, with sirens, exploding shells, and the rain of bombs getting closer and closer.

The finale came a little after eight o'clock, when three small incendiaries landed on Kobe House spewing napalm through the roof areas. There was surprisingly little panic or even wounding during the initial blasts. Some of the POWs suffered minor injuries, though not so their Japanese guards three of whom later died from extensive burns. But with flames spreading through the buildings the prisoners didn't wait for orders and evacuated down the stairs and out through the steel doors. These doors were normally secured from the outside, keeping the men locked inside the building. Luckily, if that's the right word, the blast from one bomb had blown the doors open enabling hundreds of men to escape out into the yard.

Within the hospital, the doctors and orderlies divided into two evacuation and first-aid teams. Boyce led one team of medics, whilst the other team, made up of McGreen, Florence, Denton, and another orderly, Puddifoot, were led by Longbottom. And the spare orderlies, those who were not routinely living and working in the hospital, came up to help with carrying the stretcher cases and removing equipment outside.

The POWs took what shelter there was using the small slit trenches dug into the earth, and volunteers went back to Kobe House in time to rescue some of the food from the storeroom before the flames totally engulfed the building. Back on the field the doctors and orderlies tended to the minor burns amongst the POWs. They also did what they could for the three Japanese guards who lay dying on stretchers, ignored by their own medical services.

Then for the next few hours, like extras awaiting their cue in some surreal drama, the POWs lay untouched on the ground watching the world exploding around them. Falling bombs carried on the process of razing Kobe's industrial facilities, the anti-aircraft guns continued barking shrapnel into the sky, and the prisoners looked on almost blissfully as the fires quite literally melted the bricks in Kobe House's grand finale. It was a release, an emotion, a catharsis that they had waited two-and-a-half long years to experience and now they savoured every flame-lit satisfying moment.

Later in the day as the light started to fade more armed Japanese soldiers arrived, and the POWs were marched up into the hills. Denton and the other orderlies shepherded the walking patients along, including one American and two British psychiatric cases, plus William Ellender and two other men carried on stretchers. What a whirl of emotions must they have felt as the long column of men headed away from the still burning shell of Kobe House. Given their history, they might be forgiven for feeling a sense of joy, though they were experienced enough to keep such thoughts well hidden from their guards. Though, as they trudged north towards the hills, it was surely a sobering experience clambering through streets littered with dead animals, burning debris, and the shattered bodies of civilian collateral damage. And at times, perhaps when passing the charred body of some unfortunate child, many of the men wondered if their Army escorts' automatic weapons were intended for a bloody retribution once they reached some quiet and hidden place up in the hills.

The POWs eventually arrived at Maruyama on 6th June, after a weary ten-mile march through the night. Maruyama was a vermin-infested former POW camp reopened to rehouse the Kobe House POWs, plus the patients from Kobe POW Hospital which was destroyed in the same raid as Kobe House. The orderlies did their best for the sick men once there - though Company Sergeant Major Ellender, who Denton and pals had nursed for the last few weeks, died later that afternoon from inflammatory heart disease brought on by malnutrition and one or more of the infections and parasites that dogged the POWs.

Tired and hungry, the POWs tried to get through the rest of the day as best they could. Many men had lost what little kit they'd had in the evacuation of Kobe House. Two of them, Australian soldiers, Signalman Bruce Sheriff and Sergeant Alfred Stringer, needed to find a rice bowl – so they went into the kitchen to look for one. They were seen by a Japanese Army guard and the situation immediately spiralled out of control, as the two men discovered they had broken a camp regulation. The circumstances, the bombing of Kobe House and just arriving in a new camp, these things counted for nothing, and the beating, led by Furuya, began.

Allegedly, Sergeant Major Morita also took part in the torture of Sherriff and Stringer. But the relationship and degree of co-operation between Morita and Furuya was pretty much broken by this stage of the war. Morita had amply demonstrated that [within the mores of time and context] he was measured and reasoned. Whilst the wildly out of control Furuya had made his dislike and contempt for Morita plain, and it's difficult to see the two men taking part together in this atrocity. Furuya found it hard to understand how [in his view] Morita could allow the POWs to insult him [and by implication the Japanese Army] and felt that Morita did not act like a soldier. Anyway, Denton and many of his fellow entertainers at Kobe House certainly believed Morita *not* to be implicated in the torture of Sheriff and Stringer, as events would later show after the war had ended.

Whilst the detailed accounts of Sherriff and Stringer's punishment differ, essentially half a dozen guards, led by the Pay Sergeant, began a savage punishment that would last for hours. The guards who helped Furuya were also from Kobe House and well known to the POWs. They all had their POW designated nicknames. Private Tomizo Hanamori was known as 'Horse Face.' Private Akira Otaki was called 'George Formby,' because of a resemblance to the British comedian and film star. Superior Private Takeo Kanamaru had the alias 'Gentleman Jim,' whilst Private Masaji Yamamoto was nicknamed 'Betty Boop' after the female cartoon character.

But the funny nicknames are where the humour abruptly stops. The guards stood around Sherriff and Stringer, who of course, had to stand to attention. Led by Furuya, the senior rank present, the guards used sticks to beat the two men around the head and body, they kicked them, thrashed them using heavy army issue belts, punched them, and even threw heavy stones at them. When the two soldiers collapsed unconscious, the guards threw buckets of water over them, revived them, and renewed the assault. Finally, their hands were tied behind their backs and they were suspended from the branch of a tree with their feet only barely touching the ground. Then they were left hanging there for a few hours, Stringer with a broken jaw, Sherriff's face sliced open in numerous places, both men bleeding, bruised, and battered.

Few men witnessed the beating, as all the POWs had been ordered back to their huts before it began. And when Stringer and Sheriff were hanging from the tree, Denton and the other orderlies were still powerless to do anything and had to wait until the men were cut down before they could attend to their injuries.

Over the next couple of weeks a sort of routine reasserted itself, the cooks used their limited supplies to prepare two small meals a day, occasional working parties were taken down into Kobe to labour on what was left of the docks and factories, and the orderlies nursed the sick. For Denton, probably the highlight of this time was watching from his hillside vantage point as the smoking napalm fuelled city broiled when the American air force returned to Kobe on 15th June. But, in a world at war, one man's highlight is another man's nadir. Perhaps then, for the Japanese guards, driven out of Kobe by American bombers, watching their city burn from the best seats in the hillside stalls, the ongoing destruction of Kobe was the last straw that spurred them onto their final acts of brutality.

Not long after this Warrant Officer John Barron incurred the Pay Sergeant's wrath when he contravened some sort of rule or regulation. In return, Furuya spent a quarter of an hour punching and slapping Barron around the head and face. Then he had Barron stung up by the wrists, to the same branch of the same tree that Stringer and Sherriff had been tortured from, with his feet only barely stretching to touch the ground. And for the next eight hours Barron was left hanging, trying to support the weight of his body on outstretched toes, hungry, thirsty, holding on to the pain from broken teeth in a bruised and bleeding face.

Some days later, on 19th June, one hundred and twenty-three men, mainly Australians, but including around nineteen British POWs who were too sick to march, were sent to Nomachi [Camp Nagoya 10b]. Many friendships, not to mention some musical acts, were torn apart by this. One of these men sent to Nomachi was Bill Poulter, who had sung in a small choir with Denton, Florence, and a couple of other men. The rest of the POWs, including Denton, went to Wakinohama, and were billeted in the dormitories of a former American school.

Moving down to Wakinohama was popular with nobody, neither prisoners nor guards, given that it was located back in Kobe City, next to a big iron foundry in the industrial area. The journey there must have been a bitter-sweet experience, the long column of men picking their way through rubble strewn roads and then passing close by the ruins of Kobe House. Looking up, Denton was able to see the iron door from the safe room hanging over the gaping chasm where the floor of the hospital had been – the room where he had spent so many long days and nights amongst the sick and the dying. But reflections and philosophising were luxuries better left for the future, the immediate priority for the POWs arriving later at Wakinohama was organising themselves into the dirty cramped portion of the accommodation that had been allocated to them.

They spent the next few weeks at Wakinohama on decreasingly short rations, with work parties going out daily to the remains of Kobe's docks and factories. The doctors and orderlies set up a little hospital, and the decrease in food quality, and the stress and anxiety brought on every time the air-raid sirens sounded, effected an increase in disease and illness that kept them all busier than they would have wished. But for the men going out on the work parties, aside from the opportunity to scavenge for food, the benefit was access to information. And news of the atomic bomb dropped on Hiroshima on August 6th soon filtered through from the Japanese civilians to the POWs. Of course, no one knew with any certainty just what the lethal potential of these new bombs was. And the reports filtering in of mass widespread destruction from a single bomb, tempered any satisfaction they felt with well justified fears for their own survival. But, three days later, Russia declared war on Japan and the American air force dropped an atomic bomb on Nagasaki – and, so, it was over

On August 15th the Emperor of Japan addressed his people via the wireless and announced the nation's surrender. The Japanese guards and officers, none of whom had ever even heard the emperor's voice before, gathered around the radio set, some with heads bowed, others stood at attention, whilst the emperor instructed them to endure the unendurable. Most of the POWs were out on working parties. But those prisoners who were left in camp, including Denton and the orderlies, watched on from a discreet distance with both comprehension and incredulity seeping in and wondered, until a little while later the interpreter came up to the hospital and confirmed the news that Japan had surrendered and that the war was over.

The role of the Japanese Army guards henceforth was to ensure the safety and welfare of the POWs, an incongruity that was lost on no one. Almost overnight roles reversed, and the guards began to salute the POWs. Food and the Red Cross medical supplies that the Japanese had previously refused to issue out, were now handed over. Men could walk to the latrine without fear of being beaten up for some minor or imagined infraction of the rules, sit and talk to each other, take a drink of water, and so on, freed from the brutally enforced layers of rules and restrictions that had dogged their lives for so long.

Many of the men left the camp against advice and [understandably] went into the areas of Kobe not previously torched, searching for food and beer. Others preferred to spend some time in quietude and reflection. Letters were written, plans were made, dreams allowed to re-surface. It made sense again to believe the unbelievable.

Denton released *his* angsts in a more direct way. He sought out Furuya, the Pay Sergeant, the man who had tortured so many defenceless prisoners and, in soldiers' parlance, 'read his horoscope.' Denton punched Furuya to the floor and started smacking his head against a rock, until being dragged off by some of his pals. Then, leaving him with the words 'you're not fit to be a sergeant major,' Denton ripped off Furuya's three-star badge of rank (which Denton's grandson has to this day).

Given Furuya's history at Kobe House, and the degree of hatred that the soldiers felt towards him, he was lucky that anyone intervened to save him. And Furuya, hoping to be forgotten, then disappeared faster than a politician's promise after an election, though a War Crimes Tribunal issued a harsh reminder a couple of years later.

But Denton had concerns aside from revenge. Denton, Flo Florence, Mr. Goat, and the rest of the concert performers had banded together over the last couple of years as prisoners, friends, and entertainers. So, during this strange hiatus, as the

Japanese relinquished their controls over them prior to the arrival of Allied forces on the ground, once again they did the thing that had sustained them perhaps more than anything else, and joined up with men from other camps and planned a grand concert performance for their comrades. The concert was scheduled for Monday evening on 27th August, and a rehearsal was held that day during the afternoon using a theatre in part of the building that had survived the bombing. Now, few entertainers are happily upstaged, but, when planes from an American aircraft carrier flew overhead, they readily dropped everything and ran outside to join the mass of excited men waving up to the circling aircraft.

One of the planes dropped a message of encouragement telling the men that it wouldn't be long until help arrived and, as promised, the following day food and supplies were parachuted over the camp. So, it must have been a truly buoyed up concert party that went on stage at 6 p.m. that evening and performed, not just in front of their comrades, but with an audience of allied and neutral civilians come in from the surrounding area.

Performing, singing, joking, acting skits and sketches, without the fear of beatings or even torture, inevitably buoyed up both performers and audience. High spirits prevailed, even more so off stage, and some of the British officers were brought back to camp to keep a lid on the actions of the men. One of the officers, Captain Mann, from the Middlesex Regiment, and a survivor of the *Lisbon Maru*, like Denton and many of the other POWs, took over full command of the camp from the Japanese. And at 9.00 a.m. on Friday, 24th August 1945, Lance Bombardier Denton stood to attention amongst the Royal Artillery detachment, as the whole camp paraded outside on the main road to watch the hoisting of the Union Flag.

As military ceremonies go, it wasn't exactly Horse Guards Parade and the Trooping of the Colour. Uniforms were ragged, and in some cases unrecognisable. The band consisted of one man playing a clarinet. And, as a mark of respect and comradeship to the small contingent of American servicemen, the Stars and Stripes was hoisted first to the accompanying tune of the *Star-Spangled Banner*. Some of the fine detail of that day is unclear now, but the process is time honoured and predictable. The senior NCO, probably Warrant Officer Challis, shouted the order, 'Parade, Parade – [Atten] 'Shun.' Immediately, every man on parade came to attention whilst the Union Flag was slowly hoisted up the flagpole and the lone musician played *God Save the King*.

The thoughts of every man there were both different and the same, relief that the ordeal of captivity was over, dreams of home and family, hopes for the future, grief for absent friends - men long entombed in the *Lisbon Maru* or others crushed, broken-bodied, into a wooden barrel for cremation at Kobe House. But to be sure, as the flag touched the top of the pole and the last notes of the anthem died out, there was no shortage of pride and likely more than one or two watering eyes. Then, Captain Mann no doubt addressed the parade, and there would have been a prayer, before the men were dismissed to retire into the crowded makeshift barracks where the inner demons that would never leave most of them sat, patiently, waiting for the quiet times…

Repatriation began in September when an American officer arrived at the camp and the men were taken by train to Hammamatsu, showered, de-loused, and issued clean uniforms. Before they left, Morita, the enemy who had beaten more than one or two of them, and the friend who had supported their concerts and earned a reputation for fairness, came to say goodbye. He came to the railway station and Denton was amongst the former POWs who shook his hand and wished him well, something that would have happened to very few prison camp guards in Japan.

Some former POWs were repatriated by air, including a few of the Kobe House men, though the majority were transported home via the sea. So inevitably many men were separated from their pals, and Scouse Maher, who'd been at Denton's side during the *Lisbon Maru* sinking and later at Kobe House, was sent off in a different group.

Seven former Kobe House prisoners were flown for one leg of the journey as passengers onboard an American B24J Liberator bomber, nicknamed 'Ginny.' They all died along with the crew when the plane crashed on 10th September: amongst them was Major Houghton, who had been Denton's commanding officer for most of the time he was at Kobe House. Less than an hour later, three more former Kobe House men died when another Liberator bomber, 'Les Misérables,' crashed into the sea (though five other men were picked up by a warship that was in the area).

It was a rotten and impersonal absurdity for any man to have survived massacres and imprisonment but then be killed in an accident whilst travelling home. News of the crashes soon spread, though specific details were vague. It was saddening news, made worse for Maher who was under the impression that his pal Denton had been on one of the crashed planes. In fact, Denton was amongst a group of men taken by sea to Leyte, in the Philippines, where they embarked upon an American transport ship, the USS Admiral Hughes and then landed in Victoria, Canada, on 9th October.

After a train ride from Victoria, Denton sailed from Halifax, Nova Scotia, aboard the *Île de France*, a former French ocean liner commandeered after the fall of France and converted into a troopship. After being treated so well on the first leg of their journey home, Denton, like most of the POWs being transported, was dismayed at conditions below decks. The POWs were given hammocks to sleep in on crowded messdecks, and the promised medical facilities were conspicuously lacking. The upper decks and the recreation facilities were reserved for officers, civilian passengers, and V.I.P.s, which was predictable for the time, though resented, nonetheless.

Perhaps what hit them the hardest though, and even more so psychologically than physically, was the food rationing. But Denton had initially sailed onboard a United States Navy ship and then transited across Canada. Both those nations had abundant food supplies, and the USA's economy had boomed because of the war. So, both individual kindness and state largesse was aided by a foundation of relative plenty. Great Britain, however, by this time teetered on the edge of economic collapse, and the population, both civilian and military, had experienced years of tight food rationing themselves. And arguably, in further mitigation, the previous years had strewn out individual miseries and horrors on an industrial scale, and most people had little real concept of how just how badly the Far East POWs had suffered.

THE FINAL ACT

The *Île de France* landed three and a half thousand former POWs in Southampton on 31st October 1945. Aside from it being Denton's birthday, this was his first sight of England, his home, since being posted to his regiment in Hong Kong in 1937. Given his experiences over the previous years, one can imagine what an emotional day this was.

After various medical and admin formalities most of the men were sent home on leave. Though few of them travelled home unaccompanied - the demons, eternally patient, had re-patriated themselves along with their hosts, always ready to join in concerto with the residuae of tropical disease and lingering malnutrition and strike at the former POWs.

Most men suffered illnesses (and many died early from them) ranging from relapses of malaria and amoebic dysentery, ischaemic heart disease, tuberculosis, liver cirrhosis caused by previous hepatitis B infections, peptic ulceration, osteoarthritis, hearing impairment, nutritional neuropathic syndromes, including optic atrophy and painful sensory peripheral neuropathy, and so on. Tropical diseases and parasites also persisted decades after the war, with around a third of the ex-POWs suffering from, for example, *Strongyloides stercoralis*, better known as the nematode worm. And aside from the physical effects, probably a third or more of the former POWs experienced some degree of Post Traumatic Stress Disorder – and far too many of these men took their own lives, unable to live with their memories.

For Denton, aside from hearing problems and some of the other relatively minor POW ailments, it was heart disease and cancer. Florence suffered from lingering intestinal issues that later evolved into cancer. Whilst Maher, arguably the most harmed psychologically, was later to cry out for help in the most spectacular manner.

Denton travelled to his family home in Rotherham to find that his father had died years earlier, the house had been sold, the money was gone, and his siblings and relatives long gone too. It hadn't been the closest of father and son relationships, but bereavement and homelessness wasn't quite the return that Denton had envisaged. There was nothing Denton could do about it, events, death, life even, were outside his control – a lesson writ large in the sinking hull of the *Lisbon Maru* and the dying winter of Kobe House. What was really left to him now was how he viewed things, how he responded, *his* thoughts, *his* actions.

Four months later, Denton married Margaret, a member of the Women's Land Army. The couple had twin girls, who both died within days of birth, then in 1948 they had a son. The son survived, the marriage didn't, and they divorced a few years later. Denton's career in the army had finished long before this too. He'd left in 1946 with few regrets and even fewer accolades, his discharge papers stating that he was reliable, of good character, and that during his service he had 'performed duties of a general nature.'

One might think that the phrase 'duties of a general nature' was pushing understatement rather too far, when applied to a man who had fought in the battle for Hong Kong, helped pump water from the sinking hulk of the *Lisbon Maru*, risked his own health to nurse his dying colleagues, and organised and performed in morale boosting concerts inside a brutal prison camp for which services he'd had his skull broken by a convicted War Criminal.

There was, of course, no intent to personally slight Denton. By this stage the army had demobilised around one and a half million men, so no surprise that sometimes the process was somewhat impersonal. And Denton's former regiment was no longer in existence, the officers who knew him long dispersed, as were those from Kobe House who might also have spoken out on his behalf. The result being that the discharge papers ended up written by an officer at 175 Heavy Regiment RA, where Denton was sent for discharge. So, an officer who only knew Denton for six days wrote his bland certificate of conduct, with no meaningful records to base it on and knowing little of the sinking of the *Lisbon Maru* and Joe's actions whilst in captivity.

Meanwhile, Florence, who was discharged through the RAMC, was awarded a Mention in Dispatches, whilst Flynn, the senior NCO at Kobe House hospital, was awarded the MBE. If more of the facts had been known, then perhaps Denton might also have been recognised in some way too. Though, like most every former prisoner of war, he was more concerned with adapting to home and freedom than worrying about awards. Divorce, unemployment, illness, an inability to settle, alienations from life itself, were commonplace amongst former prisoners of war. Many men found resolution eventually though, whether healed through time, understanding, medication, psychiatry or, in some cases, by suicide.

But the best thing left them was the friendships, the bonds forged in war and the prison camps. Some veterans, whether by temperament or circumstance, buried their past in a deep place along with the concomitant ties of friendship. Many, though, turned back to the men who understood as only those who had passaged through the same gate could. And for Denton, there was perhaps one man who more than any other encapsulated his connection to this brotherhood, and that was Flo Florence, the man who had been by his side almost day and night during imprisonment at Kobe House.

In 1965 Denton met a girl, Valerie - some twenty years younger than him. They immediately scandalised local society by marrying, and then defied the naysayers by having a blissfully happy marriage and raising three children. They also moved to Canada, as a family, but returned to England in the early 1970s when Denton partnered in opening a butcher's shop. Then, at age fifty-nine, Denton had a heart attack and had to give up working. Ever one to make the best of a situation though, Denton took advantage of the opportunity given him by enforced retirement to renew his search for his old pal, [Scouse] Maher.

The war had finished with Maher believing that Denton had died along with some other Kobe House POWs onboard one of the planes that had crashed whilst flying men home. So, naturally, he wouldn't have looked in Denton's direction for help during his own psychological crisis. In 1949 Maher had been living in Liverpool. He was married, had two children, and had been employed as a nurse at Rainhill Mental Hospital - but had left and subsequently taken a job as a bus conductor in Birkenhead. Then, one morning, three days before Christmas he put an unloaded Luger pistol into his pocket and took the ferry from Birkenhead to the Pier Head in Liverpool. Whether he walked or took the bus up from the Pier Head to Tarleton Street isn't clear. But, regardless, he went into George Clitherow's jeweller's shop, pointed his pistol at the old man and told him to open-up the safe or he'd be shot. The man refused, and then Maher ran out of the shop straight into the arms of a plain clothes policeman who happened to be walking past and had heard Clitherow calling out for help.

Seemingly, Maher was experiencing financial, housing, and possibly domestic troubles. But the court recognised that the real cause of what we would now recognise as Maher's PTSD sprang from events a decade before in the Japanese prison camps. Mr. Justice Oliver, a judge who had sent men to the gallows before, was no soft touch. But he was also a veteran himself, and a holder of the Military Cross. And Oliver ordered that the psychiatric treatment Maher had been getting whilst on remand be continued, saying to the prison doctor, 'I will put him back in custody and you will look after him.'

Years later, knowing nothing about his friend's misadventures, Denton travelled to Liverpool still searching for Maher. Getting on a little in years now, suffering from illnesses with implications that he was experienced enough to understand, Denton, as we do when looking towards the end, was really travelling backwards making sense of memories that refused to fade. So many friends and comrades never left the *Lisbon Maru's* hold, left behind in the blackness whilst Denton and Maher had escaped together. And few people would have the insight, or the right even, as Maher would, to discuss and perhaps answer the undeserved yet inevitable guilt-questions – why did *we* survive, what was it all for?

Sometimes Denton would take his son to Liverpool with him and they would walk around likely places hoping to pick up some word of Maher's whereabouts. Denton even placed advertisements in the newspapers, though to no avail. The scent of wild strawberries, or perhaps more appositely, Strawberry Fields, eluded him - and both Denton and Maher would go to the grave, so much unsaid, so much unanswered, each thinking the other already lost or dead.

Over the years Denton and many of the other men who he'd lived, laughed, feared, survived, and triumphed with during harsh captivity at Kobe House would meet up. Drinks, songs, chatter, old boys sat together in some Working Men's Club, with few of those around them knowing, and none perhaps understanding, the dramas, the history that forged them as one. When wives or outsiders were present it was social, but *the* conversations, the journeys back to a dark place were exclusive – the price of membership something one is glad not to have paid. But often too the banter was light, much shared laughter as when Johnny Inglis recounted how he'd had to be restrained and locked in a room whilst Japanese dignitaries had visited the power station at Sellafield where he was working. Another time, Denton, Florence, and Inglis got up to sing at Ollerton Working Men's Club and you could hear the proverbial pin drop. So yes, there were plenty of good times too.

A second heart attack hit Denton in the mid-nineteen-eighties. His family sat with him through the night as doctors pulled him through. He survived, though there were other illnesses - all part and parcel of the POWs' health legacy that left them suffering long after many of their former captors had been rehabilitated. Some men became embittered or campaigned for reparations, boycotted Japanese goods, and railed about the convicted Japanese Army war criminals who had long been pardoned and rehabilitated whilst they continued the slide along the road of physical, and sometime psychological, decline.

The 1971 goodwill visit to the United Kingdom by Emperor Hirohito - the man Denton and Florence had bowed to in enforced respect whilst this 'Son of Heaven's' soldiers starved and abused them - had felt like a stab in the back. Perhaps more personally affronting than the Emperor's reception in the UK though, was the issue of men like Tatsuhiko Furuya, Kobe House's former Pay Sergeant, who had tortured POWs, and broken Denton's skull: Furuya had been convicted of war crimes but had later been amnestied and released from prison.

Yasuji Morimoto, the camp commandant at Kobe House had been convicted of 'command responsibility for [numerous] atrocities committed by his subordinates' upon the POWs: Morimoto was also amnestied and released from prison in 1957. Colonel Sotaro Murata, who had overall command of camps in the Osaka area, including Kobe House, had been charged with causing the deaths of POWs by making them work whilst they were ill and failing to provide adequate food and medical care. Murata had also been charged with causing the death of Private Everett Tyler, the American soldier who had been tortured and then murdered by lethal injection: Murata was also eventually amnestied and released.

It's hardly surprising then that a sense of injustice, anger, hatred even, lingered amongst Kobe House's former inmates. But Denton's pals also shared a sense of fair play, and in a twist of fate they ended up coming together to defend one of their former guards at his war crimes trial. Two years after the war, Sergeant Morita, the camp sergeant major at Kobe House, had been put on trial for his role in the prison camp system and had also been accused of taking part in the torture of Sherriff and Stringer. Morita's wife, in desperation, had written asking for help and support in her husband's defence. In response, the general feeling amongst the men that Denton remained in contact with was that whilst Morita had been no soft touch, he'd treated men fairly within the realities they'd all lived within.

Nick Helliadis wrote pointing out Morita's role in supporting the POWs' morale boosting concerts. John Welford recalled that it had been Furuya he'd seen beating Sherriff and Stringer and reminded the court that Morita had been junior in rank to Furuya, and hence powerless to prevent any of Furuya's excesses anyway. Norman Colley [Mr. Goat] wrote a letter from a sanatorium, where he was being treated for tuberculosis caused by his time as a POW, saying how Morita had often helped the concert party and turned a blind eye to breaches of the rules if he was the only guard that had witnessed them. Leonard 'Bung' Owen told, as did others, that Morita only punished men when there were clear breaches of camp regulations and that punishments were [by Japanese Army standards] proportionate and measured. He also pointed out that Morita had intervened on occasion to protect [Denton and] the concert party from arbitrary punishments.

Finally, Henry Short recalled how after the end of the war, on the night that the POWs had left Kobe, that Morita had come to the railway station and that many men had gone over to Morita and shook his hand and said goodbye. Unlike many former Japanese Army guards - men like Furuya and Miyatake, the Mad Doctor, who went into hiding, fearful for their own safety - Morita was able to look his former prisoners in the eye and say goodbye. And the handshakes from *these* men was as powerful a validation of Morita's character as any trial judges' decision might have been. Yet, and perhaps more importantly, it was also a testament to the power of friendship and the fact that humanity that can flourish and survive against all odds even in the worst of circumstances.

Undoubtedly though, the deepest, most meaningful bond of friendship throughout Denton's post-war life, was that between himself and Florence. And it became even more profound and important to both men during their fading years. They met often, and to the observer seemed almost like twin souls, innately, instinctively, aware of each other's thoughts and feelings.

Like many former Far East POWs, Florence suffered from intestinal problems, a consequence of years of malnutrition and disease whilst in captivity, which in his case developed into bowel cancer. *The* phone call came in 1985, and Denton and his wife, Val, drove across to Mansfield just as they had done so many times previously on happier occasions. But this time Florence lay in bed, and Denton went upstairs to Florence's bedroom followed by Val who waited outside the room.

Both men had faced down death before in battle, then whilst trapped in the battened down holds of the sinking *Lisbon Maru*, and later side by side through the grinding years of captivity struggling to keep themselves alive whilst also caring for their sick and dying comrades. There can be no pretence with men like this. Denton sat on the edge of the bed, took his friend's hand, and they thanked each other for their friendship and for having had the honour of knowing each other. There was nothing maudlin or plaintive, no railing against death, just a quiet proud affirmation of the love and comradeship that life had forged, and that death would now extinguish. Denton leaned forward and the two men hugged and then shook hands, and once again thanked each other. It was a proud goodbye in a very British stiff-upper-lip tradition that has faded away itself along with the men of character that upheld it.

In 1993 Denton was diagnosed with terminal cancer, given what the doctors calculated as a three-month prognosis. Unable to work and distressed about the financial hardships his family was experiencing, Denton followed the advice of one of his former POW pals and applied for a war pension, which was only granted, eventually, five weeks before his death.

Joe Denton soldiered on for another two years, contemptuous of any diagnosis, until the harsh physical realities spoke plain, and on the 25th July 1995 he died. Battling and defiant, he'd taken larger and larger doses of morphine to fight the pain. But he'd struggled to stay on his feet for long enough. His final words now, to his beloved wife, 'Val, I'm not scared of dying, I'm just scared of leaving you.' And so it was done, the final act in a life well lived.

AFTERWORD

In writing this account I have drawn upon a mixture of sources including official documents and publications, both published and unpublished memoirs, eye-witness accounts, letters, newspapers, and personal interviews. Sometimes these sources differ slightly regarding chronology, in other instances they flatly contradict each other whether factually or interpretively in respect to certain incidents and characters. The construal of all this information, detailed and relevant in places, scanty in others, and sometimes mutually contradictory, has been my own. And I've drawn it all together to paint the picture as seen primarily through Joe Denton's life and experiences. Inevitably, then, there are gaps in the narrative whether because the information no longer exists or because other events, no matter how important in the bigger picture, wouldn't have been within Denton's more personal remit.

I hope that it's clear now that this account is not presented as a conventional history book. Nonetheless, I've portrayed events and personalities as honestly and as accurately as possible, given the limitations of source and the erosions of time. I've tried, as best I can, to bring it all to life, to paint a picture, to draw the reader emotionally into what I believe Joe Denton thought, felt, and experienced. Whether or not I have succeeded is for you to judge.

◆ ◆ ◆

I would also like to acknowledge my gratitude to Steve Denton, who has conducted extensive and scholarly research on the topics of both Kobe House POW Camp and the sinking of the Lisbon Maru. Steve's advice and input has been invaluable in writing this book.

Readers who are looking for a comprehensive historical account of either the battle for Hong Kong or the sinking of the *Lisbon Maru* might do well to turn first to Tony Banham's books which can be accessed via his website, the Hong Kong War Diary.

THE ENTERTAINERS

The Mad Gang

Colley, Norman. Corporal. 2070595. Royal Engineers.

Helliadis, Nicholas H. Private. 6202746. Middlesex Regiment.

Welford, John. W.O.II. 1868430. Royal Engineers.

Thorne, Reginald A. Stoker Petty Officer. P/K46936. Royal Navy.

Short, Henry E. Petty Officer. C/J40659. Royal Navy.

Jefford, Albert N. Lance Corporal. 1874087. Royal Engineers.

Kennedy, Charles. Private. 3054479. Royal Scots.

Owen, Leonard V. Private. 3054937. Royal Scots.

McDougall, James. Private. 3053495. Royal Scots.

The Harmony Three

Denton, Joseph. Lance Bombardier. 860406. Royal Artillery.

Florence, Francis E. Corporal. 7262906. R.A.M.C.

Haines, Thomas. Private. 6208244. Middlesex Regiment.

IN MEMORIAM

Kobe House POWs who died whilst in captivity.

W.O. Jupp, John E. H.K.R.N.V.R. 12.10.42
Pte. Dixon, Arron H. 6210892 MX. 16.10.42
Pte. Jones, Harry G. 6202789 MX. 16.10.42
Capt. Cuthbertson, Norman H. 74594 R.S. 17.10.42
W.O. II Hobbs, Frank W. 1860696 R.E. 17.10.42
Boom Eng. McFarlane, John C. R.N.R. 17.10.42
Cpl. Taylor, Guy. 1874426 R.E. 17.10.42
S/Sgt. Wilson, George F. 1862768 R.E. 17.10.42
Sgt. Booth, James. 2874392 R.S. 18.10.42
Pte. Ferris, Stanley R. 6201181 MX. 18.10.42
Spr. Fountain, Alfred M. 2014599 R.E. 18.10.42
W.O. Crabbe, William G. H.K.R.N.V.R. 20.10.42
Lt. Col. Stewart, Henry W. 9005 MX. 21.10.42
Cpl. James, Charles 1871384 R.E. 22.10.42
Spr. Dexter, David C. 1874684 R.E. 24.10.42
Maj. Innes, Leslie W. 22631 R.E. 24.10.42
C.P.O. Bater, Harold C. D/M37318 R.N. 25.10.42
Q.M.S. Ford, Albert E. 1865943 R.E. 25.10.42
P.O. Watts, Thomas P/J14612 R.N. 25.10.42
Lt. Philips, Eric G. 146774 R.A. 25.10.42
Sgt. Tavendale, Ian R. 833477 R.A. 27.10.42
Pte. Harrison, Edward 6202330 MX. 28.10.42
Pte. Myles, James 3055407 R.S. 30.10.42
R.S.M. Goodfellow, Isaac 3050915 R.S. 31.10.42
Pte. Sach, George 6198387 MX. 31.10.42
Pte. Cohen, Norman 6203958 MX. 31.10.42
Pte. Harvey, John B. 6200684 MX. 6.11.42
Pte. Butterfield, Edward 3055692 R.S. 7.11.42
L/Bdr. Stafford, Arthur J. 853211 R.A. 7.11.42
Pte. Sandell, Alfred A. 213002 MX. 9.11.42
Gnr. Thompson, Charles C. 1438819 R.A. 12.11.42
Pte. Phillips, Joseph 3054068 R.S. 13.11.42
Pte. Miller, Charles A. 6202863 MX. 14.11.42
L/Cpl. Harlow, Harry 3059154 R.S. 15.11.42
Pte. Searle, Alfred E. 6214365 MX. 15.11.42
Pte. Sinclair, Alexander G. 3063759 R.S. 17.11.42
Cpl. Park, Hamilton W. 3053694 R.S. 18.11.42

W.O. II Beamont, George R. 1865764 R.E. 24.11.42
Pte. Ranson, Eric 6200793 MX. 26.11.42
Sgt. Betts, Charles 5769666 MX. 28.11.42
W.O. II Gales, Christopher 1859679 R.E. 1.12.42
Cpl. Crichton, Thomas E. 3050013 R.S. 12.12.42
Gnr. Eddleston, William H. 1492736 R.A. 13.12.42
Spr. Shephard, George B. 1877730 R.E. 14.12.42
Ab. Smn. Bull, Francis C. D/JX 19857 R.N. 17.12.42
Cpl. Meakin, Frank 6207916 MX. 24.12.42
Pte. Elliott, Harry G. 6203907 MX. 27.12.42
Commander *O'Brien, Thomas F. U.S. Navy 29.12.42
Pte. Eaton, Walter T. 836184 MX. 29.12.42
Pte. Gray, George J. 6202108 MX. 2.1.43
Sgt. Woods, Frank J. 845902 R.A. 6.1.43
Cpl. Davis, Frederick J. 6194972 MX. 17.1.43
L/Cpl. McAlarney, Joseph 3054207 R.S. 17.1.43
L/Cpl. Hughes, Leonard 6207586 MX. 18.1.43
Pte. Slann, Frederick A. 6210552 MX. 23.1.43
Cpl. Blackie, Arthur 3054165 R.S. 24.1.43
Capt. Hilton, Frank W. 71817 R.A. 27.1.43
Pte. Sheehan, Martin 6202103 MX. 30.1.43
Stoker P.O. Smart, Stanley G. D/KX 81418 R.N. 1.2.43
L/Cpl. Day, Reuben, J. 1874426 R.E. 5.2.43
Pte. Patullo, David 3053616 R.S. 7.2.43
Pte. Gardner, George A. 6201661 MX. 8.2.43
Spr. Payne, Sidney 991421 R.E. 11.2.43
2nd Lt. Matthews, Vivian R. 146689 R.A. 13.2.43
Pte. Root, Alfred E. 6203948 MX. 14.2.43
Capt. *Merchant, Frank E. U.S. Army 17.2.43
Lt. Cheesewright, Cyril 149468 MX. 17.2.43
Pte. Edgar, Robert 3054528 R.S. 18.2.43
Pte. Toothill, Robert 3059144 R.S. 20.2.43
2nd Lt. Waulkden, Alan F. H.K.S.R.A. 23.2.43
Pte. Lamb, Joseph P. 6210636 MX. 28.2.43
Pte. Greig, Joseph 3055733 R.S. 2.3.43
Pte. Gray, Ian 3055728 R.S. 3.3.43
P.O. Skinner, Sidney A. C/JX 132691 R.N. 3.3.43
Lt. QM. Bowes, George W. R.S. 4.3.43
Pte. Gordon, Robert J. 7518982 R.A.M.C. 4.3.43
Boom Eng. George, Frederick C. Civilian. 6.3.43
Pte. Miller, Alan 3059019 R.S. 6.3.43
Pte. Duff, Joseph 3054089 R.S. 8.3.43
Pte. Huggett, John 6213513 MX. 9.3.43
Constable. Tyrer, Robert F. 60 R.N.D.P. 10.3.43
Sgt. Fraser, William 3049325 R.S. 11.3.43
Cpl. Painting, Robert 6200827 MX. 12.3.43
Lt. QM. Maxwell, Andrew R.A.M.C. 13.3.43
Pte. Parker, James E. 6202344 MX. 20.3.43
Cpl. Hardy, Cyril T. 1871443 R.E. 21.3.43
C.P.O. Andrews, William H. D/JX 163086 R.N. 22.3.43
Gnr. Tubb, Cecil 6394452 R.A. 22.3.43
Pte. Moyes, Henry 3054403 R.S. 26.3.43
Pte. Wilderspin, Harry 6201867 MX. 26.3.43
Pte. Jones, John 6198827 MX. 28.3.43

Pte. Sullivan, William 6213591 MX. 30.3.43
Cpl. Dyne, Charles 2075873 R.E. 5.4.43
Sgt. Fox, William R. 5989045 MX. 5.4.43
S/Sgt. Neubronner R.E. 8.4.43
Chief Stoker. Gardiner, Leslie J. D/K 56061 R.N. 10.4.43
Pte. Funnell, John 6202119 MX. 15.4.43
Chief E.R.A. Jeffs, Sydney H. C/MX 46760 R.N. 21.4.43
Pte. Bindon, Frank J. 6201249 MX. 24.4.43
Spr. Fawcett, John R. 1871744 R.E. 26.4.43
Spr. Burnett, Allan F. 2191935 R.E. 3.5.43
Cpl. Cox, William T. 6199136 MX. 3.5.43
Pte. Gunn, Lawrence F. 6213499 MX. 11.5.43
Pte. Bunker, John S. 6207610 MX. 25.5.43
Cpl. Chalmers, Andrew 3054504 R.S. 2.6.43
Pte. Sturges, Albert 602743 MX. 1.7.43
L/Cpl. Toombs, Joseph H. 6208218 MX. 4.7.43
Pte. James, William A. 3054486 MX. 22.7.43
Spr. Harrison, Harold 1874428 R.E. 1.8.43
Dmr. Gough, Albert S. 3054530 R.S. 5.8.43
Pte. **Hall, Walter E.   NX2174 2/30 Bn. 15.8.43
Pte. Pegg, Charles W.   6212991 MX. 31.10.43
Pte. **Towers, Robert G. VX36974 2/29 Bn. 8.11.43
Maj. Horswell, Sydney J. H.K.D.D.C. 15.11.43
Pte. **Tysoe, Harry WX9226 2/4 MG Bn. 26.11.43
Gnr. **Davis, William M. QX7814 2/10 Fd. Regt. 2.12.43
Dvr. **Willsdon, Walter C. SX11722 4 Res. M.T. 2.12.43
Pte. **Phillips, Ernest W. NX37732 2/30 Bn. 17.12.43
L/Cpl. Linton, Victor J. 6200987 MX. 21.12.43
Spr. Fooks, Frederick John 1572958 R.E. 16.1.44
Cpl. Tibbs, John F. 2031740 R.E. 28.2.44
S/Sgt. Ross, Henry J. 7263015 R.A.M.C. 15.5.44
Pte. Collocott, Thomas L. 6207656 MX. 11.6.44
Pte. **McPhillips, Frederick S. NX37578 2/30 Bn. 14.7.44
W.O.II Ellender, William H. 1863600 R.E. 6.6.45
Pte. Andrews, James H. 6204080 MX. 30.7.45
Pte. Keeler, Alfred 6195957 MX. 15.8.45

The following [former] Kobe House POWs died when their plane [Les Miserables] crashed whilst they were being repatriated home.
Pvt. Clapperton, James 3055328 RS 10.9.45
Gnr. Clarke, John 4914894 RA 10.9.45
S/Sgt. Golledge, Gerald 1415975 RA 10.9.45

The following [former] Kobe House POWs died when their plane [Ginny] crashed whilst they were being repatriated home.
Sgt. Gilham, Sidney Frederick 6200749 MX 10.9.45
Sig. Harrington, Desmond M. 2323399 R. Corps of Signals 10/9/45
Maj. Houghton, Afred Cecil 49563 RE 10/9/45
Sgt. James, William Richard 847074 RA 10/9/45
Pvt. King, Thomas Patrick 6213522 MX 10/9/45
Pvt. Pargeter, Earnest Arthur 6203984 MX 10/9/45
L/Cpl. Price, Charles Henry 2324244 R. Corps of signals 10/9/45

Notes

NB: Some of the men listed above died after they were sent from Kobe House to Ichioka Hospital or Osaka Military Hospital.

RA Royal Artillery
RS Royal Scots
MX Middlesex Regiment
HKRNVR Hong Kong Royal Naval Volunteer Reserve
RE Royal Engineers
RN Royal Navy
HKDP Hong Kong Dockyard Police
HKSRA Hong Kong & Singapore Royal Artillery
RAMC Royal Army Medical Corps

*United States of America
**Australia

BOOKS BY THIS AUTHOR

The Emperor's Irish Slaves

The story of the 650 Irish soldiers imprisoned in the Japanese slave labour camps during World War Two.

Over 650 Irish citizens, serving with the British armed forces, were captured when the Imperial Japanese Army attacked Singapore and Hong Kong. They suffered torture, starvation, disease, and imprisonment in bestial conditions, whilst being used as slave labour by the Japanese. Many died of starvation and ill treatment whilst building the Burma Railway. Others died of heatstroke and dehydration whilst being transported to Japan. Some were beaten to death or bayoneted.

The survivors were released and brought home at the end of WW2. But most suffered from the effects of tropical diseases and post-traumatic stress for the rest of their lives.

Spitting On A Soldier's Grave

The story of the Irishmen who deserted from the Irish Army, and joined the Allies in the struggle against fascism and Nazism during the Second World War, has been kept secret for over half a century. These men fought in some of the bloodiest battles of the war. And after the war they were all subjected to a Kangaroo Court-Martial, and condemned without representation or right of reply.

But hundreds of these men had died long before they were court-martialled. Joseph Mullally died on D-Day, 6 June 1944, fighting with the British Army on the beaches of Normandy-- a year before. And Stephen McManus had already suffered torture and starvation whilst being worked to death in a Japanese prisoner
of war camp.

And it wasn't just the soldiers who suffered. In some cases their children were taken from them, condemned in court, and sentenced to a childhood of sickening abuse in the Industrial Schools.

But throughout the book the courage and decency of the individual shines through. Gerry O'Neill risked his life with the newly formed Irish Navy, rescuing wounded British soldiers from the beaches of Dunkirk. And Nicholas McNamara volunteered to serve with RAF Bomber Command knowing it meant almost certain death. This book tells their story.

www.robertwidders.co.uk

Printed in Great Britain
by Amazon